Triumphant
Living
in
Turbulent
Times

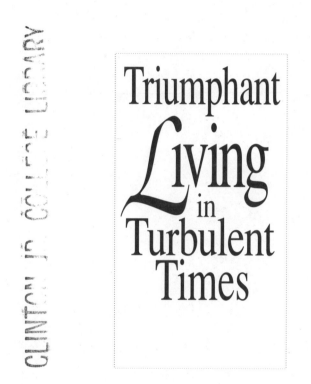

Triumphant
Living
in
Turbulent
Times

William H. Hinson

DIMENSIONS
FOR LIVING

NASHVILLE

TRIUMPHANT LIVING IN TURBULENT TIMES

Copyright © 1993 by Dimensions for Living

All rights reserved.

This book is printed on recycled, acid-free paper.

Hinson, William H., 1936–
    Triumphant living in turbulent times / William H. Hinson.
        p.   cm.
    ISBN 0-687-42641-3 (alk. paper)
        1. Christian life—1960–   2. Conduct of life.   I. Title.
BV4501.2.H5219   1993   92-41894
248.4—dc20   CIP

Epigraphs and Scripture quotations are from the New Revised Standard Version of the Bible, copyright © 1989 by the Division of Christian Education of the National Council of the Churches of Christ in the USA. Used by permission.

Scripture quotations not followed by references are the author's paraphrase.

93 94 95 96 97 98 99 00 01 — 10 9 8 7 6 5 4 3 2

MANUFACTURED IN THE UNITED STATES OF AMERICA

To My Mother,
Frances Humphries Hinson,
and My Wife's Mother,
Jean West Laird

Contents

Introduction

HOW SHOULD A CHRISTIAN LIVE?

───────────── 🌱 ─────────────

A recent newspaper article declared in bold letters that a huge comet is on course to collide with the earth in the year 2116. According to the report, the destruction to our planet upon its impact will be so great that the world will be plunged into the dark ages, if anyone survives. That is not the kind of good news we want to read over our morning coffee!

The truth is, our world is already experiencing destructive bombardment. Not the least of these "comets" is the constant stream of bad news. Daily we are confronted with bad news about our economy, rising unemployment, increasing crime, the breakdown of the family, the threat of AIDS, the rising cost of medical care, and continuing racial strife—not to mention our own personal problems and those of our loved ones. How does one live with any degree of security, let alone happiness, in turbulent times like ours?

The gospel tells us that we can be triumphant even in the midst of our troubles. Those of us who have faith in Jesus Christ have the resources of a great faith available to us. Christians are not exempt from the slings and arrows of this world. In some ways we feel the hurts of others more deeply than many. Through our faith we have been sensitized, taught to feel compassion; we are "others-centered" by virtue of being Christians. But through the power available to us, we not only survive our difficulties but also experience joy and peace in the midst of our tribulations.

This book is an attempt to help us discover, or remember, those qualities and attributes of faith that will enable us to live a triumphant life. It is written in the belief that we do not merely want to survive but to live triumphantly, even in turbulent times like ours.

1.

With Faith

Now faith is the assurance of things hoped for, the conviction of things not seen. Indeed, by faith our ancestors received approval. By faith we understand that the worlds were prepared by the word of God, so that what is seen was made from things that are not visible.

HEBREWS 11:1-3

In the morning as they passed by, they saw the fig tree withered away to its roots. Then Peter remembered and said to him, "Rabbi, look! The fig tree that you cursed has withered." Jesus answered them, "Have faith in God. Truly I tell you, if you say to this mountain, 'Be taken up and thrown into the sea,' and if you do not doubt in your heart, but believe that what you say will come to pass, it will be done for you.

MARK 11:20-23

Fats Waller, the famous jazz musician, wrote a Christian hymn early in his career. According to one pastor, the theme of that early hymn was "everything that is not of Jesus will go down."

I agree with Fats Waller. We cannot endure the

tribulations of this life until we learn to put our trust, our faith, in Christ.

If we could weigh the words of the Bible, we would discover that the word *faith* is one of the heaviest words in the entire Bible. We find faith in the Bible from beginning to end, and we wrestle with its concepts as long as we live. Faith marks the beginning of the Christian life.

Understanding Faith

In our day the concept of faith has distortions. A recent poll stated that 68 percent of the American people believe that if they live a good life, they will go to heaven when they die. There was no mention of faith in that poll.

As Christians know, of course, faith is a requirement that goes beyond living a good life. The death of Jesus would have been unnecessary if we could be saved through our good works.

The faith described in the Bible begins through the overtures of grace. When we become aware, through the work of the Holy Spirit within us, that the God who approaches us approaches us from the perspective of love, forgiveness, and acceptance, when we are confronted by that grace, we find ourselves repentant of all of the wrong that we have done. Out of that experience of repenting, we then are ushered into the relationship of faith. We do not repent in order to find God. In that connection, the discovery of his amazing love and acceptance brings us with great desire and yearning to surrender our priorities and take on God's priorities. That is the beginning of the life of faith.

We sometimes describe faith as the opposite of doubt. In reality, the opposite of faith is not doubt; the opposite of faith is self-centeredness, or that term toward which we have a cultural animosity—*sin*, the essence of which is self-centeredness. Many people talk about believing in God, but they do not have *faith* in God.

Many polls report that more than 90 percent of the American people believe there is a God. It is easier to believe that a God created everything that we see in this world than to blithely assume that creation simply "happened." Almost everyone believes in some kind of god. People are comfortable with the idea of a god. Many people are not comfortable, however, with the idea of faith in God, because faith is a personal relationship with a deity that brings with it life transformation. People can be comfortable with the idea of God ("I believe in a god"), but to talk about having faith in God is something else. Faith is a personal relationship in which our priorities are surrendered in favor of God's priorities, and that is threatening to many people.

As the Christian life begins with faith, even so the Christian life continues in faith. The all-encompassing, all-important condition of our lives is faith. That is who we are!

Exercising Faith

Herb Miller, in his book *How Not to Reinvent the Wheelbarrow*, talks in a very practical way about two of the implications of living with faith. He says that the Christian faith is a "mountain mover and an anxiety reducer." In other words, faith is the condition of our lives that moves mountains and reduces anxiety. The phrase "moves mountains" was a proverb in Jesus' day that meant "to remove difficulties." A rabbi who had the ability to take a complex subject and make it simple was described by his pupils as a "remover of mountains," a remover of difficulties. Jesus describes faith as a mover of mountains. Jesus said if you believe and don't doubt in your heart, you can move mountains. Faith and prayer remove difficulties.

The Bible does not so much define faith as it talks about people who exercise faith. In the eleventh chapter of Hebrews, we read that faith is the "assurance of things hoped for, the conviction of things not seen" (Heb. 11:1). This is not a definition of faith as much as it is a characteristic of faith.

The rest of that marvelous chapter in Hebrews is given over to the roll call of faith, to a description of people who have exercised faith in their lives. Chief among them, of course, was the man Abraham, who has been called "The Father of Faith." That is why, when the apostle Paul started his discussion of faith in the fourth chapter of Romans, he did not get into a theological definition of what faith is, he just told about Abraham. Abraham, who went out not knowing where he was going; Abraham, who was seventy-five years old when he received the call and didn't exactly have the young blood of an adventurer flowing through his veins. Abraham left Ur of the Chaldeans and went out not knowing where he was going. He was simply following the command of God. You might say, "Oh, Abraham was saved because he went out not knowing where he was going." No, he was saved because of the faith that was within him, the faith that propelled him to go out. The Bible says, "Faith was reckoned to Abraham as righteousness" (Romans 4:9). It wasn't what he did, but it was the faith within him that called him and caused him to move out.

Later God came to Abraham and told him he would have a son. "You ought to be excited because you are going to have a boy and he is going to be the son of the promise and in him all of the nations are going to be blessed." The Bible says that Abraham did not waver but was fully convinced that God was able to do all that he promised. He was fully convinced, though he considered himself as good as dead because he was already one hundred years old and his wife was barren. Still, he knew that God could fulfill and keep all of his promises.

How many times have you acted on a great faith like Abraham did? Sometimes our faith remains smaller than the proverbial mustard seed because we do not fully utilize the faith we have already been given.

There is a story about an old farmer who was interrupted in his plowing one day by a college graduate who was trying to sell him some books on how to farm in a more scientifically correct way. The farmer said, "I don't want any of them books." The young man persisted, saying, "But, sir, if you will use these latest scientific books, you can increase your effectiveness at least 100 percent. You can double your production." The old farmer replied, "Shoot, son, I just farm half as good now as I know how to farm."

Many times we are not using the faith that we have been given. Many times we confuse faith with understanding, but faith is not just intellectual acceptance. Many times we only attempt that which we know to be humanly possible. So, when we are assured something is a lead pipe cinch and it is within our ability to get it done, we're ready to try it, and then we wonder why we don't grow in faith. When was the last time you tried something that was impossible, humanly speaking—something that was impossible unless God came to your rescue and to your assistance?

When you read the roll call of faith you will discover that those persons have one thing that causes them to stand apart: their willingness to try that which is absolutely impossible without the help of God. It is probably a good thing for a Christian to confront a dead end early on in his or her Christian experience, to be brought to the realization that Christians are those who do not walk by sight. We walk by faith; and until we begin to walk by faith and not by sight, the Christian life isn't going to be very exciting. In our secret heart we are going to wonder what difference faith makes.

I often think about the dead end I confronted when I headed out for seminary. I had driven that old car fifty miles on "empty." When it said "empty," it wasn't quite empty, and I surely was glad. But when I parked the car at that seminary, I knew I could not crank it until I had found some money. I had only ten dollars in my pocket. I got in line to sign up for classes that day, and I confronted Helen Stowers, who was at the end of the line in order to talk about fees. When I approached Mrs. Stowers, I said, "I don't have any money, but I want to go to school. If you will find me a job, I can work." I'll remember her smile as long as I live. She not only found me one job, she found me three jobs. I remember thinking, as I drove away after finishing seminary three years later, that not only had God helped me through seminary, but he also had given me my ten dollars back.

We Christians are those who recognize that our God moves mountains. Our God opens doors and makes things happen that nobody believed could happen. We cannot always describe how. I am not sure that we even need to know how.

In the musical *The Song of Bernadette*, there is a line that says when we believe, we need no explanation; and when we do not believe, an explanation does not satisfy. Either you have been there or you haven't. Either you have been like Paul, who spent the night in a storm holding on to his faith, knowing it was there and knowing it was real, or else you have an untried faith and you aren't sure you have the wherewithal to make it through a storm. Or maybe you feel that you have lost your faith, but that is okay, because a rebuilt faith is like a broken bone when it heals. It is even stronger than it was before it was tested.

When James Michener, the author of so many epic novels, including his best-seller *Space*, testified before the Senate Subcommittee on Space Explotion, he gave the committee a little history. He spoke of the discovery that the world was round and the realization that people wouldn't fall off the edge if they sailed in one direction. When that realization surfaced, Spain and Portugal moved very quickly to begin their explorations. Italy and Germany never did. France and England came late; England made a remarkable recovery, but France did not. Michener declared in his summary that it was a matter of vision. Some saw a vision and had faith in the vision and believed that what they perceived to be in the future was indeed out there. That made all the difference for them.

Experiencing the By-products of Faith

How do we perceive our future? Faith perceives a future for us that God holds. When faith perceives a future that is held by God, we can get up in the morning even if we have lost our jobs and life is caving in on us, and we can face the day with warm expectation, because we know there is a future and we know who secures it and who brings it. We live with faith as a mountain mover. We live with faith as an anxiety reducer.

Jesus commanded us not to be anxious. That command is found in the Sermon on the Mount. Living without anxiety is not easy in our time, however. Our stress levels reach unacceptable heights, and we choke on our anxiety. During the Persian Gulf War a lot of people stayed tuned to a news station. Again and again I heard newscasters say, "Don't miss any of the news. Get all of the news." One morning as I heard them say that for the umpteenth time, I thought, *How can I handle* all *of the news?*

We have so much to be concerned about. There is war, political instability, and the national deficit. There are people breaking into our homes in broad daylight. Criminals threaten our loved ones; they steal our cars; they snatch our purses. We are surrounded by bad news. If you are given to worry, you have more to work with now than you have ever had before. Ours is a mixed-up world. How are we going to keep our equilibrium in a world like ours? Everything seems to be coming loose.

Not very long ago my wife, Jean, and I had the chance to go to Yellowstone National Park. We were very excited because we had never been there. While there, we wanted to do what four million people do every year: we wanted to see Old Faithful erupt. We went out on the boardwalk to wait for Old Faithful, and we waited and we waited and we waited. Finally, it erupted, and we certainly were not disappointed. But I thought about how you could really count on Old Faithful a few years ago. You knew that regularly, on the hour, it was going to erupt. You could set your watch by it. Then there was an earthquake, and things got unsettled in the center of the earth. Now the signs say, "Old Faithful will erupt at approximately such and such a time." As we waited out there on the boardwalk, I said to Jean, "Old Faithful isn't faithful anymore. We are going to have to change the name of Old Faithful to Old Unfaithful."

As we view our world, we have the same kind of

feeling. So many things, including things that we thought were constant and reliable, seem to need direction.

In a world like ours where we are looking for some perspective, how do we keep our equilibrium?

This is God's world, and a person of faith knows that. This is God's world, and we know what God is like because we have looked into the face of Jesus. Having seen and met Jesus Christ in a personal relationship, we know what God is like. We don't have the answers to all of our problems. I don't know anyone who does. But we certainly know God is ultimately in charge.

In an interview with Mrs. Albert Einstein, a reporter asked, "Mrs. Einstein, do you understand your husband's mathematical theories?" She shook her head and smiled and said with a twinkle in her eye, "No, I don't understand Albert's mathematical theories. But I have something better than that; I understand Albert."

We don't know the mind of God on all things. We don't claim to have all of the answers. But, as people of faith, we know God. We understand him because we know Christ, and, therefore, we will not be afraid. Though everything seems to go wrong and Old Faithful cannot be counted on, we know we belong to a kingdom that cannot be shaken—not earthquakes, not inflation, or anything else can shake us loose. When that confidence seeps into our bones, we begin to experience the by-products of faith. One of those by-products is trust. We learn to trust God.

A loving grandfather was trying to calm his granddaughter. She was anxiety ridden, and her life was coming apart at the seams. The grandfather was driving her through the countryside one day, trying to find the right words to say to her. It was in the fall. The leaves were still on the trees, and there had just been an unexpected snowstorm. As they rode along, they noticed that the rigid elm tree limbs were breaking off all over the place under the weight of the snow. Then they noticed that the evergreen trees let their branches sag, and the snow was falling off their branches. The grandfather turned to his granddaughter and said, "Granddaughter, be an evergreen. Relax, and don't let these things destroy you. Let these burdens roll off."

There is, on the part of every Christian who has saving faith, the ability to relax and know that our God will not put more on us than these fragile limbs are able to bear. We do not see into the future. We do not have any extra knowledge or greater understanding. But we have a personal relationship that has built a sense of trust within us. That is why our burdens do not destroy us.

I like the story entitled "Who Saved the Robins?" That story was about the city workers in Hamilton, Ontario, who were trimming tree limbs when they discovered a nest of robins on one of the limbs. They decided they would trim around that particular limb. After the little robins flew away, the city crew came back and took down the limb where the robins had nested. When they looked into the nest, they found a ragged, soiled piece of paper with some barely legible words: "We trust in the Lord our God." Who saved the robins? Who saves us? We trust in the Lord our God.

2.

With Self-control

Now when Jesus learned that the Pharisees had heard, "Jesus is making and baptizing more disciples than John" —although it was not Jesus himself but his disciples who baptized—he left Judea and started back to Galilee. But he had to go through Samaria. So he came to a Samaritan city called Sychar, near the plot of ground that Jacob had given to his son Joseph. Jacob's well was there, and Jesus, tired out by his journey, was sitting by the well. It was about noon.

A Samaritan woman came to draw water, and Jesus said to her, "Give me a drink." (His disciples had gone to the city to buy food.) The Samaritan woman said to him, "How is it that you, a Jew, ask a drink of me, a woman of Samaria?" (Jews do not share things in common with Samaritans.) Jesus answered her, "If you knew the gift of God, and who it is that is saying to you, 'Give me a drink,' you would have asked him, and he would have given you living water." The woman said to him, "Sir, you have no bucket, and the well is deep. Where do you get that living water? Are you greater than our ancestor Jacob, who gave us the well, and with his sons and his flocks drank from it?" Jesus said to her, "Everyone who drinks of this water will be thirsty again, but those who drink of the water that I will give them will never be thirsty. The water that I will give will become in them a spring of water gushing up to eternal life." The woman said to him,"Sir, give me this water, so that I may never be thirsty or have to keep coming here to draw water."

JOHN 4:1-15

We live in a culture where many confess, and perhaps you have said it, too, "My life is out of control. I don't know what is happening to me, but I feel as though I am coming apart at the seams." We know that it is not accidental that we have a proliferation of addictions on every side. Alcohol and drug addiction threatens to engulf our country, perhaps an entire generation of our people. When the Bible speaks of self-control, we should be very attentive. The Bible not only teaches us about self-control, but in Jesus the Bible shows us the personification of self-control.

Self-control Is Inner Strength and Composure

Jesus demonstrates in his experience of going through Samaria what self-control is all about. We see our Lord in John 4:4 indicating that he had to go through Samaria. In his willingness to do what he obviously did not want to do, he showed us that through self-control we can direct ourselves to the highest and finest that we know. In other words, we can make ourselves do what we don't want to do.

Jesus did not need another controversy. The Pharisees had already discovered that he was making more disciples than John the Baptist. The Pharisees had been threatened enough by John, and finally he had been killed. Now here is someone who is putting John in the shade, and the controversy is growing about the number of people being won to his cause. Jesus knows that unless his short ministry is going to be even more dramatically shortened, he needs to leave Judea and go on to Galilee and finish all that the Father has given him to do.

Judea was in the south, Samaria in the middle, and Galilee in the north. Jesus could have gone across the Jordan and around Samaria, but, instead, he indicated that he had to go through Samaria. Knowing the situation in Samaria, and the relationship between the Jews and the Samaritans, we would ask Jesus, "Why would you jump from the frying pan into the fire?"

Jews and Samaritans did not have anything to do with one another; there was a feud that was more than seven hundred years old. The Jews disliked the Samaritans because the Samaritans had intermarried when they were held in captivity and were no longer racially pure. There was also a dispute about the location of the Temple, and a dispute about scripture. Suffice it to say that the Jews and the Samaritans did not like one another.

So for Jesus to be leaving one controversy and going into Samaria, of all places, is not the kind of thing one would readily do. That is why we have this kind of language, "I must go through Samaria," or "He had to go through Samaria." Nevertheless, Jesus demonstrates great inner strength and directs himself to do it. He is the fulfillment of what the writer of Proverbs was talking about when he said, "One who is slow to anger is better than the mighty, and one whose temper is controlled than one who captures a city" (16:32).

We need to hear that in our culture because we have those around us who believe in the no-sweat, no-strain manner of living. The only sweat and strain they advocate is perhaps a little exercise. In terms of life's objectives as laid out by Jesus Christ, they are not interested.

The high priest marveled at the composure of Jesus. Accusations were being hurled at Jesus that would finally cause his death, and he did not even answer. When he stood before Pilate, Pilate said, "What do you have to say to these testimonies against you?" Jesus did not utter a word. And the Bible says the governor marveled and wondered at such a man. He had never encountered such inner strength and composure. Even when everyone else around him seemed to be losing theirs, Jesus stood with a composure that made people wonder at its source. He could do what he did not want to do. That is the mark of a person with self-control.

Self-control Is Overcoming Circumstances

More than that, Jesus had the ability to do the right thing even when he was not feeling at his best. Read John 4:1-15 carefully, and you see that Jesus is weary. The Bible says it was about noon. The heat must have been incredible out there at that desert well. Jesus is so exhausted that he sits down in whatever little shadow was created by that well. He waits there for his disciples to go into the city to bring him some food because they haven't eaten for a long time.

While he is waiting there at the well, a woman of Samaria comes. She has many strikes against her. First of all, she is a Samaritan; and second, she is a woman, and that does not help in her day. Third, she is a very sinful woman; she has a horrible reputation and even could be the town prostitute. This is precisely the situation where you want to pretend you don't see someone; you certainly don't meet the person's eyes.

What does Jesus do? He says, "Would you please give me a drink of water?" Jesus is asking something of her, setting aside her defenses, making himself dependent upon her. Jesus is initiating a conversation with a sinful Samaritan woman.

Now if Jesus had been on his own territory—if he had been feeling his best—and this had been just an ordinary woman, then we could imagine how he could have done that. But we know our caring is limited and our concern is sometimes superficial because people catch us at the wrong moment. Let's face it. Many of us are at the mercy of our moods. If someone asks us something when we are in a good mood, the outcome is good. But if someone has the misfortune of asking us on one of our bad days (and maybe many of our days are bad days), if someone talks to us about a concern or a need, we simply are not ready.

But here is Jesus when everything is wrong, and we can still count on him to care. When he said, "Come to me, all you that are weary and are carrying heavy burdens," he meant any time, anywhere. He did not say, "Come on my good day; come when I have just had a nice meal and a good night's sleep and everything is going right with me." He said, "Come to me, all you that are weary and are carrying heavy burdens, and I will give you rest" (Matt. 11:28).

No wonder they were threatened by him. When people have that quality of self-control, they are powerful people. People who have the ability to direct themselves, regardless of their circumstances, make an impact. They make a difference. They aren't afraid to try great things for God.

Self-control Is Not Instantaneous

The Matterhorn, that mountain on the frontier between Italy and Switzerland, stretches up into the sky, and much of it is almost perpetually shrouded with clouds because it is 14,701 feet tall. As you can imagine, many people have attempted to climb it, and some have been successful; but others have died in the attempt. There is a little cemetery in the shadow of that mountain. In that cemetery, there is a grave marker with these words: "We who lie here scorned the lesser peaks."

Surely the person who wanted that epitaph had a measure of self-control, because people who can control themselves know they can exploit themselves—if necessary, unto their death. But the timid souls who cannot try anything great cannot exploit themselves because in their heart of hearts they are at the mercies of every whim and every desire. The self-controlled person is a powerful force. But such self-control is not instantaneous; it doesn't just happen.

Look at Jesus, for instance, in terms of salvation history. His decision to go into Samaria wouldn't rank as one of his greatest decisions unless you were that woman at the well who learned of the living water. Jesus could have gone around Samaria and taken six days to go to Galilee. He saved only three days by going through Samaria. It was not a big decision, but it is the little decisions that either crumble or create our character.

Maybe it was a small thing for Jesus to say, "I have to do this," but there was going to be a day when he would say, "I have to go to Jerusalem. I have to go die on a cross. I have to go make an offering of myself for the sins of the whole world." That was the biggest decision anyone ever made. The Bible says that those who are faithful over a little will be made master over much. That is how we all grow.

Someone referred to Pablo Casals, the famous cellist, as a genius. Casals said, "Genius, nothing! I practiced for thirty-seven years, fourteen hours a day, and now they call me a genius!" We have to cooperate with God in this matter of self-control.

Self-control Is a Gift of God

When Paul wrote to Timothy, he said, "Timothy, I want you to rekindle the gift that is within you through the laying on of my hands, because God has not given us the spirit of timidity. God has given us a spirit of love and power and self-control." Self-control is a gift of God, and that is the way Christians understand it. We have to cooperate with God to have it, and we can't have it in the Christian sense apart from God.

Ephesians talks about the immeasurable greatness of God that is within us who believe. The Bible has said that God has put all things under his feet for all of those who believe. If something is tearing your life up or wrecking your home, with Jesus Christ you can put it under his feet.

I was fascinated by a footstool in the antiquities museum in Cairo. I was impressed not only because it was inlaid with all kinds of precious stones, but also because it had scenes from all the victories in that pharaoh's career. When the pharaoh sat down on his throne, his slaves put this beautifully carved footstool under his feet. Literally, he had his enemies under his feet.

When the Bible says God has put all the enemies of life under the feet of Jesus, it means and includes even the enemy of death, which is the last great enemy of all. If we will give ourselves to Jesus, yield this self that is riddled by fear and apprehension, he will give us back a self that is marked by self-control.

That is the key, isn't it? When Jesus said to those disciples who asked him why he was not eating, "I have food to eat that you don't know anything about," he taught them a lesson. He said, "You see it is my meat to do the will of my Heavenly Father. I live to accomplish his work." Jesus had an overriding purpose in his life, and everything else had to take a second seat.

We live in a society so conditioned by science that we interpret everything in terms of cause and effect. Some people say the Enlightenment made it unnecessary to believe in God; everything in the universe can be explained by cause and effect. This is not just a cause-and-effect universe. This is a universe guided by purpose. When we plug into the purposes of God, suddenly we find that all of the power in the universe is available to us through Jesus Christ.

Benjamin Fine wrote a book on the underachievers among us. He said that the basic problem with people who just can't do what they want to do is they do not have a central purpose, an overriding goal that focuses and directs their lives. That central purpose is how we get self-control.

Some years ago a Swedish immigrant was kicked off a train in Columbus, Montana. They threw him off the train because he was a hobo, a bum. They really did not want him riding their freight car. That man walked over and sat down on the bank of the Yellowstone River and took stock of his life.

He remembered how he had grown up in a Christian home. He remembered that his mother and father told him that if he did not base his life on the principles of Christ, he would not amount to anything. On that day in Columbus, Montana, he wept when he considered how far he had strayed from those teachings. Then he accepted Jesus Christ as his personal Lord and Savior and began to live according to the principles of Jesus Christ. Years later that man was elected governor of the state of Montana, and he served two terms with great distinction.

Regardless of what may have you down, there is someone who can lift you up—not only lift you up, but also give you the power to walk this earth with victory. Jesus Christ can give you the gift of self-control.

3.

With Forgiveness

Now there was a disciple in Damascus named Ananias.
The Lord said to him in a vision, "Ananias." He
answered, "Here I am, Lord." The Lord said to him, "Get
up and go to the street called Straight, and at the house of
Judas look for a man of Tarsus named Saul. At this
moment he is praying, and he has seen in a vision a man
named Ananias come in and lay his hands on him so that
he might regain his sight." But Ananias answered, "Lord,
I have heard from many about this man, how much evil he
has done to your saints in Jerusalem; and here he has
authority from the chief priests to bind all who invoke
your name." But the Lord said to him, "Go, for he is an
instrument whom I have chosen to bring my name before
Gentiles and kings and before the people of Israel; I myself
will show him how much he must suffer for the sake of my
name." So Ananias went and entered the house. He laid
his hands on Saul and said, "Brother Saul, the Lord Jesus,
who appeared to you on your way here, has sent me so
that you may regain your sight and be filled with the Holy
Spirit." And immediately something like scales fell from
his eyes, and his sight was restored. Then he got up and
was baptized, and after taking some food, he regained his
strength.

ACTS 9:10-19

Some friends in our church have two little boys who enjoy playing putt-putt. Although they have played many times, the younger of the boys, who is seven, has never succeeded in winning a game. His nine-year-old brother always wins. One day after finishing the first nine holes, the seven-year-old said to his older brother, "I'm not going to play with you anymore until you agree to give me at least three 'do overs'."

All of us need "do overs." We need them for ourselves, and we must extend them to others. Forgiveness is essential for all of us.

A Story of Forgiveness

The young man Stephen was being stoned because of his belief in Christ and because of the magnificent sermon he preached that had not been well-received by the elders. As Stephen was dying, Saul of Tarsus stood nearby consenting to his death, having been a part of his condemnation by holding the cloaks of those who threw the stones. As Stephen died, he saw the Lord Jesus standing on the right hand of the Father, and Stephen prayed that the Lord would not lay any sin to the charge of those who were stoning him.

Throughout all of these years, the church has maintained that we are indebted to Stephen for the conversion of Saul, who, of course, became Paul. It was Stephen's prayer, much like the prayer of Jesus as he died on the cross, that started Paul on the road to his own conversion experience. There is no doubt that we owe Stephen for the conversion of Paul on the road to Damascus, but we are also deeply indebted to Ananias for the completion of that conversion experience as it occurred in the house of Judas on the street called Straight in the old city of Damascus.

Ananias played a pivotal role in the life of a man who became the greatest apostle and the greatest missionary the church has ever known. Ananias was a very obscure disciple who played a cameo part in the drama of salvation. Ananias appears in the scripture briefly, without much mention having been made previously about his life and his ministry. We are introduced to him with a simple statement: "Now there was a disciple in Damascus named Ananias" (Acts 9:10a). But what a disciple Ananias was! Obviously, he was a man of prayer, for it was during his prayer that the Lord gave him the vision that he was to go and pray for Saul. When Paul later recounted the experience in his own words, he said that Ananias was a devout person and that he was well-spoken of by all people of faith in his community. So we know he was a person of prayer.

More than that, we know that Ananias was a man of great faith and that his faith enabled him to be obedient to the summons of his God. Ananias sounded like Samuel in the Old Testament, when the Lord appeared to him and called his name, for when the Lord said, "Ananias," he answered, "Here am I, Lord." It was almost as if he were reporting for duty, saying, "Lord, send me on your errand; what do you want me to do?" Of course, when he spoke so bravely and courageously, he had no idea of the nature of the errand on which the Lord was going to send him.

The Lord said, "I want you to go to the house of Judas on the street called Straight and pray for Saul of Tarsus because he has seen a vision that you are going to come and pray for him. I want you to pray for Saul that he might receive his sight and that he might be given the Holy Spirit." Ananias was not certain at this point that the Lord knew anything about Saul of Tarsus. He was not sure that the Lord was up to date on who that man was. So he began to educate the Lord. He said, "Lord, I have heard about this man, and I have heard of all the hurt that he has done to your people. Saul has persecuted the saints, and in his fanatical zeal he has murdered them. He has laid waste your church, and now he has been ordered by the high priest to come here and do the same thing to all of us."

Ananias did not know, of course, that at noonday on the road to Damascus, Jesus had appeared to Saul in a light brighter than the sun that struck Saul down and blinded him. Saul thought he was a good man. He was a Pharisee; he was a lover of God; he thought he was serving God in persecuting the church. Out of the Damascus road experience, Saul received the awful news that in persecuting the church, he had been persecuting Jesus, the only begotten Son of God.

Saul was a devout Jew who received the crushing news that instead of serving God, he had been persecuting the followers of God's only Son. Out of this experience he was made absolutely blind. He was led by the hand to the street called Straight, an old street that runs from the east side of Damascus all the way to the west side, to the house of Judas. There, he waited for somebody to come and pray for him.

Ananias did not know those things about Saul, of course, but, nevertheless, when the Lord sent him and said, "Saul is a chosen instrument of mine," Ananias went to pray for Saul. Ananias was a man marked by obedience. More than that, he was a forgiven man, because only someone who has been profoundly forgiven can begin to forgive someone who is murderous, as was Saul of Tarsus.

Obviously, God would like all of us to be like Ananias. In reality, many of us play the part of Saul. We have a form of spiritual blindness ourselves. We are in desperate need of somebody to come and extend the Lord's forgiveness to us. We are sitting there like Saul, wondering how in the world God could put us back in his good graces after the terrible things we have done. To me, there is no more beautiful and tender sight in all the Bible than when that humble, obscure disciple stretched out his hands in forgiveness to Saul.

The laying on of hands has always been a part of the service whereby one is brought into the church and into the Body of Christ. It is a gesture of friendship, used to this very day when we extend the right hand of Christian fellowship to all those who have newly come to the community of faith. There is nothing more poignant, more tender, than when Ananias stretched out his hands and touched the hand of Saul of Tarsus and said, "Brother Saul, the Lord whom you met on the road has sent me to pray for you." You don't ever forget an experience like that.

Years later, when Paul was an old man, bearing in his body the marks of all his suffering for Jesus, when he was making his defense before King Agrippa and was about to be carried off to Rome where he would be put to death, he still remembered that Ananias in Damascus had put his hands on him and said, "Brother Saul." All of the love and the forgiveness of Almighty God was tied up in that form of address.

We Experience God's Forgiveness Through Others

God doesn't have to have an intermediary to forgive us. We know that God can and does forgive us directly and take away our sins. However, many times God needs to appropriate his forgiveness through a human hand. Many times that human hand needs to be the agent that makes that forgiveness real, that gives it credibility, that interprets the forgiveness of God. Someone once said that heaven's mercies are encompassed in human hands. This meeting of Saul and Ananias divinely illustrates one of those times when heaven's mercies were encompassed in human hands.

There is a great story about the need for forgiveness in Ruell Howe's book *The Therapist.* He tells about the mother who was learning that love, if it is genuine, has to be firm. This mother had a little girl who was given to tantrums. One day the little girl was having one of those notorious fits of hers, and her mother did as her counselor told her to do; she just quietly left the room and refused to pay any attention to her daughter. That infuriated the little girl all the more. She stomped out of the room and went upstairs.

After a time, her mother heard a silence. I don't know how mothers can hear silence, but somehow they can. There are different silences—there is silence you ignore, and then there is silence you had better not ignore! The mother heard that latter silence.

She ran upstairs and there, in the middle of her bedroom, the little girl sat with the pieces of her mother's best dress. She had snatched that favorite dress out of the closet and had cut it up with scissors into tiny pieces. When her mother saw what she had done, the mother fell across the bed in tears. The little girl, moved by her mother's tears, went over and started pulling at her mother's hands, saying, "Mommy, Mommy." Finally, her mother looked at her and said, "What do you want from me now?" The little girl said, "Mama, I want you to take me back. I want you to take me back."

Somehow the little girl felt she had done such a horrible thing that she was no longer in relationship, and she desperately needed her mother's embrace and her mother's love to let her know that nothing had broken that relationship. We all need that assurance, and sometimes we need it from specific persons whom we have hurt along the way.

The story of Jacob and Esau illustrates this. It was the right of Esau, the older brother, to inherit the bulk of the estate and to be the leader of the family after the father died. There were all kinds of privileges given to the eldest in that society. Jacob, however, caught Esau at a vulnerable moment and bought his brother's birthright for a pot of stew. Jacob also tricked his father, who was almost blind, into giving him Esau's blessing. Jacob, unlike his hairy brother, Esau, had no body hair. He wrapped pieces of an animal's skin around his arms and went in and deceived his father so that his father gave him the blessing that Esau should have had.

When Esau learned what his conniving brother had done to him, he was so angry that Jacob had to flee for his life. Jacob went to Mesopotamia, married Leah and Rachel, and had a big family. After some years, however, Jacob was filled with discontent and regret. Finally Jacob headed back to Canaan and the destiny that he knew awaited him. The first job he had to do was to put things right with his brother. He was scared to death of Esau, and he should have been.

Jacob was a wealthy man by this time, and so he put together a package of presents—hundreds of sheep, goats, camels, and donkeys—which he sent on ahead. He thought that maybe after Esau saw his generosity he would not want to take a pound of Jacob's flesh. He even divided up his family. He took poor old Leah and her children and sent them out in front, calculating that if Esau was in a murderous rage, by the time he got through with Leah he might not kill Rachel, his favorite wife, and his son Joseph.

At this point, the Lord worked a miracle in his life and caused Jacob to change his plan. The next morning Jacob went out in front. He did not come along behind his family but chose instead to go out before them, despite his fear of Esau and the knowledge that Esau was coming to meet him with four hundred fighting men.

A wonderful thing happened that day. When Jacob saw Esau coming, he bowed to the ground seven times, but Esau would have none of that groveling. Instead, Esau ran up like the father in the return of the prodigal son, threw his arms around Jacob, and called him brother. Then Esau said, "I don't need all these gifts, brother. I have enough, and I don't need them." Esau fell on Jacob's neck and kissed him and wept because he was so happy to see his brother.

What did Jacob say in response? He said, "To see your face is like seeing the face of God" (Gen. 33:10). Jacob could not see the face of God until God made his forgiveness real and appropriated it through the loving, forgiving touch of his brother. Have you had that experience?

I graduated from seminary with a young man who went to serve several small churches while I went to one church. I was fortunate to have a single church on which I could concentrate my efforts. I could visit all thirty-nine members of my church every single week. The Lord really blessed that little church with some wonderful people. They matured spiritually, and the congregation grew in size to the point where we had a grand little church. We even built a new sanctuary and a parsonage with air conditioning. That was really something in those days.

In the meantime, my friend was plodding and working away with his churches. He did not have everybody talking about how wonderful things were, like I did. But an unusual thing happened. My friend got a big "promotion"; he moved on to a good-sized church, and I found myself at a little church that was smaller than the one I was serving. It was like starting over.

I began to wonder what my friend had that enabled him to get that "promotion," especially since, in my jaundiced eyes, he was not nearly as worthy as I. Dwelling on that, I began to resent him. After a time, I came to the realization that I did not have a prayer life anymore. Oh, I prayed at the hospital, and I prayed at the church, and I prayed at home, but I was not really praying. I could not see God's face anymore. I had lost the joy of serving, and I was not getting anything out of my ministry. I knew no one else was, either.

Finally, the Lord convicted me, and I got in my car and went to see my brother. He did not know what I was talking about; he did not even have the foggiest idea. I said, "You have got to hear my story because I have been thinking bad thoughts about you. Every time your name is brought up, if I have the opportunity, I say something derogatory about you—just a little cut and a little criticism. I am here because I desperately need your forgiveness. I have got to get right with God."

My friend forgave me, and that day marked the beginning again of the ministry of prayer in my life. I tell you that looking at his face when he said, "I don't understand any of this, but I forgive you," was to see the face of God.

We Are Called to Forgive Others

There are people reading this who need to be forgiven. You are sitting in the house of Judas on the street called Straight, and you are looking for some Ananias to say, "It's all right; I love you, and I forgive you." Then, once you are forgiven, the Lord wants to make you like Ananias. He wants you to be an extension of his love and forgiveness in a hurting, separating, alienating world.

How did the Lord encourage Ananias to be so forgiving? Read that story and you will see that Ananias agreed to go when the Lord told him that Saul of Tarsus was a chosen instrument who was going to preach his word to the kings, to the sons of Israel, and to the sons of the Gentiles. There is something sobering about the Lord reminding us that he has a plan for the life of the person that we most enjoy disliking. He has a plan and he has aspirations for the person you most enjoy disliking. God comes to us as he came to Ananias and says, "This person is a chosen instrument; now are you going to help me or are you going to hinder me? Do you want to see my will done in that person's life or not? Are you going to be a stumbling block or are you going to be a helper?"

This little resentment is not confined to you and the person you resent. It involves your God, and it is a sobering realization to know that first you must hurt God before you hurt anybody else. It is tough to forgive, I know that. It is tough to be a "forgiver" because when we begin to forgive people, we surrender our moral superiority. We get down on the same level and acknowledge that we, too, are sinners who have been forgiven. We acknowledge that we have also tasted of that cup. It costs something.

It is almost impossible for us to forget. Our God can forget sins against him, but we cannot forget sins against ourselves. We are called to forgive them even when we remember. I know that is tough. I understand that. But the power of God working within us can help us be forgiving people.

We lived near the beach when our children were just beginning to go to school, and we enjoyed many a happy day with them there. One day one of our children who had just learned to print his name enjoyed doing so in the wet sand. He became frustrated, however, when the waves came in and washed away his name. He finally asked me, "Where can I write so the water won't wash my name away?" I explained that he would have to write his name beyond the place where the water reached.

When we write our sins, through honest confession, and put them within the reach of God, there is a tide of forgiveness that comes and relentlessly washes them away. Like the onrushing waters, God's love erases our transgressions.

How did God do it with Saul and Ananias? He gave Saul a vision that Ananias was coming. He gave Ananias a vision to go to Saul. That was a double vision.

Dr. Conrad of Boston, a distinguished pastor of another era, had a church member who kept a running vendetta against him. A series of poison pen letters, mysterious calls, vicious gossip, and the like were constant reminders to him of this particular

woman's opposition. She even began an open move-
ment to have Dr. Conrad dismissed from his church.
After a number of years, the woman finally moved
to Arizona to be with her daughter. Shortly after she
arrived in Arizona, the woman had a powerful experience with Christ and dedicated her life to him. She
wrote Dr. Conrad, asking for his forgiveness. Dr.
Conrad telegraphed the woman because that was the
fastest means available to transmit a message across
the country. His telegram contained three words:
"Forgiven! Forgotten! Forever!"

Dr. Ernest Campbell, while pastor of the Riverside
Church in New York City, preached a sermon in
which he told a story about retired Bishop Donald
Tippitt. Bishop Tippitt's left eye drooped severely.
The story of that eye went back to Bishop Tippitt's
earliest days as a young pastor.

One day when the young Donald Tippitt was in
his study, two young thugs entered his office and
beat him up with brass knuckles. In that experience,
he received the permanent injury to his left eye. The
young men were tried and convicted for their
crimes. Young Donald Tippitt, however, pled for
them and visited them regularly while they were
incarcerated. After their release, he helped one of
them through college. The former convict eventually
completed medical school and became an ophthal-
mologist.

Forgiveness changes lives. Our lives are changed
as well as those who are the recipients of our forgiveness.

4.

With Peace

"I have said these things to you while I am still with you. But the Advocate, the Holy Spirit, whom the Father will send in my name, will teach you everything, and remind you of all that I have said to you. Peace I leave with you; my peace I give to you. I do not give to you as the world gives. Do not let your hearts be troubled, and do not let them be afraid.

JOHN 14:25-27

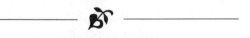

The *Houston Chronicle* carried a story in the fall of 1991 about a dramatic invention for the fire trucks and other emergency vehicles in the city. The city can now acquire, at a cost of $16,000 per unit, an amazing invention for each emergency vehicle. The invention will turn all of the traffic lights green as an emergency vehicle approaches an intersection. Can you imagine having nothing but green lights all of your trip? Throughout your life?

There is nothing in the Christian faith that promises us nothing but green lights. Life is filled with stops and starts, and some of them are tragic. But we are promised as Christian believers that the gift of peace given by Christ will make everything all right whether the light is green or red.

Sometimes when a prominent person dies, we hear people crassly inquire, "How much did he leave?" When Jesus of Nazareth died, he left very little of this world's goods. Indeed, even the clothing on his back, which was about all that he had, was taken by the squad of soldiers who saw to his death. Still, he was not without a bequest. Just prior to his death, he gave his disciples a gift that not only would *sustain* them in their troubles but would also enable them to *triumph* in the midst of difficulty. He gave them his peace (John 14:27).

Peace, of course, is the legacy of every Christian. Jesus' listeners would not have been startled when he first offered them peace, because the word *peace* was often on the lips of persons in that society. When persons met on the road, for instance, or in the town or village, they often saluted each other by saying, "Peace be unto you." Then, as they were about to leave each other, they would say again in departure, "Peace be unto you." This is why Jesus' words to his disciples after his resurrection, "Peace be unto you," had a very familiar ring.

We have adapted those words somewhat since

ancient times. At one time Christians said, "May God be with you," when saying good-bye. Today *good-bye* is a shortened form of that ancient prayer. But when they spoke of peace in the time of Jesus, it was a special wish for God's shalom, the finest that God could give.

A Peace Not of the World

Jesus gave his peace to his disciples. We should note first that the peace of Jesus is not the peace of the world; rather, it is the peace of the Prince of Peace. The world seeks peace, but the world offers a different kind of peace than the peace of Jesus.

Because we are, to some degree, products of the world, we have a tendency to go through this life thinking that if somehow we could just get our stuff together we could have peace. If we could be a success in our business or in our vocation, if we could make lots of money, if we could just indulge ourselves and do the things we like to do, then we could have peace. That is a vain hope.

I had lunch with a man at his country club. He had the money to buy the club and more if he had chosen, but he said to me as we talked, "There has to be more than this." Jesus was talking about the "more" for which every person longs when he said, "My peace I give to you. I do not give to you as the world gives" (John 14:27). The world speaks of peace in terms of escape or entertainment or diversion, or sometimes even denial. That is why, in our society, we dare not be quiet or still.

I was in a waiting room not long ago and I looked around at the magazines. The newest one was three years old. It was not old enough to be interesting as an antique and not new enough to be worthy of reading. I sat there, just being comfortable with myself, but the receptionist kept saying, "Don't you at least want me to turn on the television?" I said, "No, I really don't want you to turn on the television." She came back on two other occasions and said, "Are you sure?" I must have looked really miserable!

We are addicted to noise and entertainment. We are actually afraid to be quiet. Somehow the prospect of being entertained brushes over that void that we have in our souls. In London they have fewer than a dozen channels on their television sets, but we Americans would never accept fewer than thirty-six. Suppose we did not like what we found on channels 2, 3, 4, 8, 9, 10, or 15. We need lots of choices. We have to have some options. It isn't enough to have one football league; we have to have more than one. We have to have year-round entertainment because we have an addiction to action.

It's no secret that I like sports. Jean, my wife, once said to me, "Your problem is that you like *all* sports." I even played mumblety-peg when I was a boy. There is nothing wrong with liking sports, but there are some of us who are compulsive about it. Rather than merely acknowledging these compulsive feelings, we need to begin to look behind them to what is creating the feelings.

I read about a woman who divorced her husband because he was always watching the all-sports channel, day and night. Finally he promised that, on a certain night, he was going to turn off the television and act like a regular member of the family, but he broke his promise because a dart tournament came on and he had to see who won. The darts were the last straw, and she divorced him. Entertainment—we have to be entertained! Consequently, we are a society filled with excitement but lacking peace.

The Way to Peace

Not long ago I saw a man walking down the sidewalk wearing a T-shirt with these words written across the front of it: "Dazed and confused." I guess we ought to give him credit for being open, because at least he acknowledged his feelings. This man was not unlike the man who went to Daytona Beach just to get caught up in the standing crowd of thousands and thousands of people at the Daytona 500 car race. He stood there with all the people cheering as the cars roared around the track, and finally someone heard him utter a loud expletive. Then he said, "Everywhere I go, there I am." You know, that is true. You simply can't get away from yourself.

All of us are selves whom God shaped and molded, and God has breathed into us the gift of his own spirit. When our lives are a denial of who we are, no wonder we have all these gaps and blanks that we try to fill with everything under creation. Augustine's statement comes from an understanding of scripture: "Thou has made us for thyself, O God, and our souls are restless until they rest themselves in thee." We are never completely together until we are in God. The marvelous thing about Jesus' promise to give us peace is that we can have the peace of Christ right now, even in a dazed and bewildered world.

Rufus Jones, American educator and religious leader who authored a series of works on the history of Quakers, said that the blessed people of God, who have the peace of Christ, are not those who have just been successful in avoiding trouble. They are not just nervous Pollyannas who manage to keep their lives clear of conflict. They are not passive people; they are positive, active, creative, and powerful people. They simply have discovered that peace is not contingent on external conditions. External circumstances do not take away the peace of Jesus Christ. Nothing in this world can take away that peace. We don't have to wait until the six o'clock news to learn whether or not we are going to have peace. We can live today with the peace of Jesus Christ in our hearts.

How do we live with this peace? We remember that Jesus said, "My peace I give to you." In other words, we allow Jesus to come into our lives, and peace comes with him. I know people who desperately want all of the gifts of Christ. But instead of looking for the giver who brings the gift, they look instead for the gift; and so they miss it altogether. You cannot separate Christ from his gifts.

If you read John 14:22-25, you will see exactly what I mean. Judas, not Judas Iscariot who betrayed Jesus but another Judas, asked Jesus one day, "Lord, why are you talking about the fact that you are going to manifest yourself to the believers but not to the entire world?" I believe Judas was thinking, "You started a good action here when you rode into the city on the back of a donkey. You were beginning to make public who you are. Why are you only going to manifest yourself to the believers?" And Jesus spelled it out to him, saying, "Those who love me, keep my commandments. If you love me, you love the Father, and we will come and make our home with you."

In other words, there isn't any need to talk about God manifesting himself to someone who does not believe. Jesus explained this in the sixteenth chapter of Luke when he talked about the rich man and Lazarus. Jesus said, "Listen. They have the prophets; they have the preachers; they would not believe even if someone rose from the dead and told them." If anyone has the desire to know, that person will know. If we have a will to believe, if we have a heart to believe, then we are those to whom Christ will manifest himself.

Scottish preacher Ian MacLaren said that a Christless heart is as restless as the tossing sea. Likewise, the revivalist Sam Jones said that he thanked God he had never known a satisfied sinner. None of us is satisfied. But unless Christ comes, we will never know his gifts. We cannot separate Christ from his gifts. We must accept the claims of Christ if we would enjoy his gifts.

Many of us would like a kind of "jacuzzi Jesus"— an experience that leaves us relaxed and warm with a bubbly feeling all over, an experience that makes us feel good when we step out of it. But that is to want what is not possible to give. For Jesus does not give any of his gifts until we first accept the Redeemer.

Paul said, "Therefore, since we are justified by faith, we have peace with God through our Lord Jesus Christ" (Rom. 5:1). First we have to surrender our lives. There is only one way to peace. We must not count anything external as our own, and we must commit our all to God. In that yielding, and only in that yielding, is peace.

Recently I attended church services in another city, and after the service someone came up and startled me by saying that she had been a member of that congregation when I preached my second sermon. She had a picture to prove it. When I saw her picture of me when I was eighteen, I knew it was true. She had been there.

Since recalling that day, I have remembered portions of the sermon. I remember, for instance, talking about going through life's journey and coming to a fork in the road. One way, the right way, is narrow and steep and often difficult. The other way is easy and broad. The only problem is that instead of leading to life, the easy way leads to destruction. The more I reflected on that sermon, which I preached before I went to college, the more I realized that I really have not progressed much beyond it.

I still believe that it is this choice that determines whether or not we have the peace for which the whole world is hungry. We decide every day by choosing God's way or our own way. Only in yielding to God's way do we discover what his peace is all about. When Mother Teresa accepted her Nobel

Peace Prize, she said that unless we are full of God we cannot give peace to others.

As I continued to reflect on this sermon, I remembered one thing that I did in preparation for writing it. I went to see my grandfather. I asked Granddaddy to pray with me about finding some inspiration and some material I could use in my sermon. I remember how my grandfather prayed for hours. When I was a young boy, I would always go to sleep during his prayers, but now I was all ears because he was praying for *me*.

That night I had a very unusual dream. It was a dream that is quite vivid to me to this very day. In the dream I saw anxious parents sitting in the waiting room of a large hospital. I saw in the operating room their little girl who had been terribly hurt and was at the point of death. Beside her was an eminent surgeon who had been flown there from another continent. No expense had been spared. The family, filled with anxiety, had said to that surgeon, "Do whatever you must do, but save the life of our child."

Then, in this wonderful dream, the face of the surgeon became the face of the Master Physician. Christ himself stood beside that little girl. The parents suddenly possessed a composure and peace that was unlike anything this world could ever give.

I awakened the next morning to the realization that I would spend the rest of my life reaching toward the objective God had given me through my grandfather's prayers and through that interesting dream.

You see, I knew that if we are to have God's peace,

if Christ himself is to empower our lives, then we must yield to him. We must yield not just once but every day. Again and again we must yield to him, just like those parents who gave their child to the physician. That is the key to peace. Jesus assures us that we can have peace even in the midst of a mixed-up, bewildered world. He tells us that because he leaves his peace to all believers, we are not to let our hearts be troubled or afraid (John 14:27).

Keeping Peace

You may be thinking, "I tried to yield to God, and for a little while I had peace; but then I got that old troubled heart, and all of those old fears came back on me." Sometimes we try to do it on our own, and we forget that Christ, through the Holy Spirit, is going to help us keep the peace.

Someone has described the gift of peace as the "warrior peace." Perhaps that is because when Paul talked in Philippians about the peace that passes all human understanding, he said that peace will *keep* your hearts and minds through Christ Jesus. The Greek word for *keep* is a military word. It is the same word for *garrison*. In other words, God will, through Christ, garrison your heart and mind so that you might have peace. That is a far cry from trying on your own to be a peaceful person.

God's gift of peace is not contingent on our vain efforts. Our God, through his Holy Spirit, will garrison us if we let him. In our yielding, we receive the peace that passes all human understanding. It transcends human knowledge. There is no peace in the world that can compare with the peace of Jesus Christ.

I was reminded of that recently in an unforgettable way. A few years ago I walked with a family to the graveside when they committed a son, still in his thirties, to Almighty God. Just recently I walked again to the cemetery with this family when their last child, another son still in his thirties, was also committed to God. As I saw the mother's composure and as I could only imagine the grief she was feeling, I asked her, "How do you do it? How do you go on?" She said, "Bill, God in his mercy has given me a precious peace that tells me that my sons are with him and it is going to be all right."

If you will yield yourself and if you will yield those whom you love to Christ, you will have the peace that passes human understanding.

5.

With Contentment

I rejoice in the Lord greatly that now at last you have revived your concern for me; indeed, you were concerned for me, but had no opportunity to show it. Not that I am referring to being in need; for I have learned to be content with whatever I have. I know what it is to have little, and I know what it is to have plenty. In any and all circumstances I have learned the secret of being well-fed and of going hungry, of having plenty and of being in need. I can do all things through him who strengthens me. In any case, it was kind of you to share my distress.

You Philippians indeed know that in the early days of the gospel, when I left Macedonia, no church shared with me in the matter of giving and receiving, except you alone. For even when I was in Thessalonica, you sent me help for my needs more than once. Not that I seek the gift, but I seek the profit that accumulates to your account. I have been paid in full and have more than enough; I am fully satisfied, now that I have received from Epaphroditus the gifts you sent, a fragrant offering, a sacrifice acceptable and pleasing to God. And my God will fully satisfy every need of yours according to his riches in glory in Christ Jesus. To our God and Father be glory forever and ever. Amen.

PHILIPPIANS 4:10-20

Some of the bowling alleys in our large cities are now equipped with inflatable gutters. Those bowling alleys invite people to come and bowl with them because there will be no more gutter balls. Every single ball that is rolled knocks down at least a few pins.

It is appealing to be guaranteed some success in bowling. Such bowling, however, is not the way life is. All of us roll "gutter balls" from time to time. We must discover the secret to contentment whether we roll a gutter ball or a strike.

Paul's letter to the Christians at Philippi is basically a thank-you note. It is really more than a note, though; it is a rather lengthy letter. After thanking the Philippians for sponsoring him in his missionary endeavors, Paul quickly moves into some teaching and then some preaching. Before long the thank-you letter becomes a real epistle that gives instruction to us even today.

When Paul comes finally to the last chapter, he remembers the original purpose of the letter and says again how much he appreciates the Philippians' support. Before he finishes his gracious words of gratitude, he says, "Not that I am referring to being in need; for I have learned to be content with whatever I have (Phil. 4:11).

When you consider that Paul was writing the letter from prison in Rome and was going to be set free from prison only by his martyrdom, when you consider the deprivations and the disappointments that he was experiencing, that statement about Christian contentment is nothing short of miraculous. Even so, it is the legacy of every Christian to live a contented life.

How in the world can we be content in a time like ours? When every day presents another series of shocks and surprises—from assassinations to hurricanes to earthquakes to crime at home and abroad—how in the world can we be free of anxiety, frustration, and anger, which mark so much of what we do and what we are? Perhaps this verse stands as a lofty aspiration for today's Christian.

What Contentment Is Not

Maybe we ought to start by thinking about what contentment is not. Christian contentment is not what the Stoics had in mind. The Stoics were those who trained their minds to reach the point where nothing mattered. They started with the smallest thing, such as breaking a piece of glassware. They trained themselves to say, "It doesn't matter; I don't care." Then if they lost a pet or an animal on the farm, they would say, "I don't care; it doesn't matter." The Greek word for being content means self-sufficient. The Stoics were trying to reach the point of self-sufficiency so that nothing mattered and they needed no one and nothing.

Paul adopted that pagan word: contentment. When the Philippians realized that Paul had adopted a pagan word, they must have been startled. However, he brought another element to it. The kind of contentment Paul referred to is not what the Stoics had in mind. It was not "just grin and bear it."

Neither does Paul use *contentment* in a way that is similar to fatalism, which is a part of many world religions. I saw some of that fatalism first-hand as I traveled in Egypt through rural villages along the Nile. In one location, a perfectly fine barracks formerly occupied by government agencies stood absolutely empty. We asked our guide why those poor people did not move into the better homes, and he explained by saying, "There is the idea that if Allah had wanted them to live in a house like that, they would have been born into it." They believe it is the will of Allah to stay where they are. That is fatalism.

Doris Day is known for singing "Que Sera, Sera," but Christians don't believe this. We have never accepted "whatever will be, will be." It is tough to read the gospel, which is dynamic and full of hope and promise and change, and come away with a belief in fatalism. Fatalism is not the kind of contentment Paul is talking about.

Circumstances Cannot Bring Contentment

The kind of contentment Paul is speaking of in Philippians is independent of circumstances. Paul had experienced life from one end of the spectrum to the other. He said, "I know how to abound; I know how to be abased. I know how to have abundance, and I know how to have nothing. I know how to be full, and I know how to be hungry. I have gone from one end to the other, and in every state I am content."

I suppose there is some profit to having experienced both ends of the spectrum. Some have speculated that Paul was a wealthy man prior to his conversion experience. He speaks from experience when he talks about abundance and abounding. It is profitable to experience both and then discover that neither defines who we are as Christians.

I have experienced to some degree this phenomenon of having plenty and then too little. There was a time in my growing-up years when my father was well off—not rich by standards then or now, but certainly comfortable. I remember how he designated me as driver, and I would go to the bank to secure the payroll on Saturday. I would add up the payroll, and my father would say, "Now you are to get plenty of bills and some change so we can be exact in paying all of our workers."

Early on, I discovered that my father would let me keep the leftover change. Well, every Saturday I had enough change to make change for the whole county. Both pockets would be full! My father was a very generous person. He had plenty, and he wanted all of us to have plenty. He wanted his boy to have money in his pockets to do those things he enjoyed doing. It was wonderful.

Then I saw at our house, as so many families see, a change in fortunes. I remember still a very poignant conversation I had with my father when he was dying. I assured him he did not have to worry about who was going to pay the hospital bill; I knew some of us would find the money to do that because nobody wanted him to die anxious about his debt.

For those of you who have experienced plenty and for those of you who know something about want, I hope you are finding out by this time that you are not defined by either circumstance. We are talking about a contentment that no circumstance can change. That is the kind of contentment Christians are supposed to have. That is the kind of contentment we really want.

Our Search for Contentment

Why is contentment so hard to come by? Is it because our desires have been dispersed? Do we want everything under the sun? Is it because we don't have any unifying principle such as "Seek first the kingdom of heaven"?

I remember a picture in *Life* magazine depicting two old mules standing in adjacent pastures. Each had his head stuck through a hole in the fence, and each was eating out of the other's pasture. To be discontented is to be torn between two decisions. Some people can be torn by many, many others.

I remember a story about a Sunday school teacher who talked about Dives and Lazarus. Dives was the rich man who fared very well in this life but who, when he died, went to hell. Through all the years of his life, there had been a beggar named Lazarus at his gate. Dives had never once recognized Lazarus, much less tried to help him. When Lazarus died, however, he went to heaven.

The teacher inquired of her Sunday school pupils, "Now, which of these would you like to follow?" A little boy raised his hand and responded, "Well, I would like to be like Dives while I am alive and like Lazarus when I die."

Isn't that the way we are? We limp between two opinions.

James said, "The double-minded person is unstable in all of his or her ways." We are very unstable because we are like the wind. There is not an element of dependability because there is nothing cohesive that focuses our energies and brings them to bear on one united purpose.

Why is it hard for us to find contentment? Are we looking in the wrong places?

I remember an old story I heard so many times when I was a boy. It is not so funny now, but then it was. It is the story about the man who had too much to drink and was under the street lamp, crawling around on his hands and knees. Someone came by and said, "What are you looking for?" He said, "I have lost my keys." So the second fellow got down and crawled around with him, and after a while he said, "Are you sure this is where you dropped them?" The inebriated man said, "No, I dropped them down at the end of the street, but it is dark down there."

In other words, we must not only seek the Lord while he is near; we must seek the Lord where he can be found as well. Our society is looking for contentment in all kinds of addictions, whether it is alcohol or drugs or sex or food. We are looking for the fulfillment of ourselves in things other than God, and we are not finding it.

There was a man who subscribed to a religious

magazine. It carried a guarantee that if you were not satisfied with the paper at the end of your one-year subscription, you could get your money back. The man wrote to the editors at the end of a year and said he was unhappy with the paper and wanted his money back, but rather than putting them to all the trouble of sending it back, they could apply it to next year's subscription.

I see this kind of thing happening all the time. I see people who are trying something and are not happy with it. So what do they do? They want some more. It is like the definition of a fanatic. A fanatic is someone who, having lost sight of a goal, doubles his or her effort. Sometimes we think that if we are getting something and it is not making us happy, maybe we just need some more of it. But the more we seek contentment in *things,* the more discontented we become.

Contentment Comes Through Christ

What is Christian contentment? Paul used a pagan word that meant self-sufficient, but he added something that changed the entire meaning of the word. Paul wrote, "I have learned to be content with whatever I have" (Phil. 4:11). Then in verse 13 he wrote, "I can do all things through him who strengthens me." Pascal must have been thinking about that verse when he said, "There is a God-hole in every one of us, and stuff it as we will with things, only the Lord can fill that hole."

I had a professor in seminary who illustrated that

concept when he talked about our creation. He said that God made us; we are not biological accidents. God made us. He breathed into us the very breath of life—he imparted a portion of himself. To illustrate his point, my professor held up a rubber ball and continued, "You cut that rubber ball in half and separate it, and that is our fallen state." Then he said, "Instead of putting the two halves together again, instead of coming back to God, we try to fill up our lives with everything else but God."

The essence of sin is to try to complete ourselves apart from God. It never works. There is a limit to everything. We may have all the money in the world and all the power and prestige, but we still are not complete.

Somebody asked J. Paul Getty, who was believed to be the world's first billionaire, "How much money do you need?" He said, "A little bit more."

There is a limit, you see, to what any material thing can do. That is why the apostle Paul cautioned the Christians. He did not denounce wealth; he just said that you must be generous. If you have plenty, you'd better give plenty of it away. He said that you should not put your trust in wealth. Don't center your life around it. It is too limited.

What does Paul mean? You brought nothing into this world, and it is certain you will take nothing out of this world. We cannot give ultimate significance to anything that is limited to this small span of years. We just can't do it. We will never find contentment there.

There is a fable of a king who was sick with a very painful illness. While suffering from that ailment, he sent for the wise men of his kingdom to come and give him their prescriptions. These wise men said, after some days of consultation, "You need to find a contented person in your kingdom and wear that person's shirt day and night for a month." So the king sent the wise men to find a contented person. They were gone for many days, and when they came back, it was obvious they did not have a shirt. The king said, "Could you not find one contented person in this entire kingdom?" They said, "Yes, your majesty, we found a contented man." He said, "Well, then, why didn't you bring me his shirt?" They answered, "He doesn't have a shirt, Master."

Christian contentment is not dependent on our external circumstances. Life will never be full and life will never be satisfying until it is a Christian life lived according to the will and the purpose of God. Life is incomplete until Christ is in you, giving you himself, his strength, his guidance, and his direction.

There is a story about Earl Stanley Gardner, who, before he started writing the Perry Mason mysteries, wrote Westerns. He was paid three cents per word to write them, and his editor noticed that every time Gardner's heroes had a shoot-out, it took six shots to kill the villain. The editor said, "Look, your hero is supposedly the fastest gun in the West, the best shot in the whole world. How come it takes him six shots to kill the villain?" Gardner replied, "I am never going to finish my story as long as my hero has fifteen cents of unexploded ammunition in his gun. The story isn't over until the gun is emptied." Gardner wanted to finish the story.

There is a need within every person to somehow feel that our stories are finished, that our lives make a difference. We need to know that we have made a contribution and that we have not just strolled across this stage for sixty, seventy, eighty, ninety, or one hundred years and then disappeared as though we had never lived. Every person wants his or her life to count for something. The only way we can know for sure that our lives are whole and complete is to be in the will of our God.

Some years ago, Leontyne Price, the Metropolitan Opera star from Laurel, Mississippi, dropped out of the Met for three years and did not sing at all. When she went back to sing, someone asked, "Why did you come back?" She said, "I have recaptured the joy of singing, the feeling that courses through my body when I know the tone is right and my whole being vibrates with it."

As someone who was made by God, your whole being will never vibrate with the thrill of being right—you will never be in the position where you are supposed to be or live the life you are supposed to live or be the kind of person you are supposed to be—until you yield your life to Jesus Christ. We are content and we are satisfied and we are self-sufficient when we are Christ-sufficient. That is the secret. What we are talking about is not another technique. We are talking about a faith relationship.

I discovered that anew one night in a hotel waiting to give a lecture at a seminary. I was very anxious about that lecture. I was feeling very inadequate, and I was pacing the floor. In other words, I was coming apart.

Finally, remembering that I am a preacher, for heaven's sake, I opened my Bible and I found that passage in Hebrews that talks about being content with what you have. It gives the reason for our contentment: Christ's promise that he will never fail or forsake us. That means we live in the faith the apostle was expressing when he said that our God is able to meet all of our needs through the riches of Jesus Christ. I don't know how they graded me on that lecture, but I felt pretty good about it. I was reminded of where our satisfaction comes from.

I was reminded of the source of our satisfaction again last week by a friend who has gone into the ministry. She came to my office to tell me about her ministry. Three years ago she left a fine job to be a pastor in another state where she could take care of her mother and father, who are not well. After three years, she is making a little bit more than poverty wages. Her car has 135,000 miles on it and is still running like a top. I saw an exuberance in her face and moisture in her eyes when she talked about her people and her ministry. As I was preparing a sermon on contentment, a sermon had actually come to me. She described real contentment.

Where does contentment come from? You don't have to go into the ministry to find it. Contentment comes from knowing that wherever God has put you, you are doing his will. When you yield your life to Jesus Christ, you know that he is the only one who can fulfill your life and give you a reason for living.

6.

With Humility

Then Jesus said to the crowds and to his disciples, "The scribes and the Pharisees sit on Moses' seat; therefore, do whatever they teach you and follow it; but do not do as they do, for they do not practice what they teach. They tie up heavy burdens, hard to bear, and lay them on the shoulders of others; but they themselves are unwilling to lift a finger to move them. They do all their deeds to be seen by others; for they make their phylacteries broad and their fringes long. They love to have the place of honor at banquets and the best seats in the synagogues, and to be greeted with respect in the marketplaces, and to have people call them rabbi. But you are not to be called rabbi, for you have one teacher, and you are all students. And call no one your father on earth, for you have one Father—the one in heaven. Nor are you to be called instructors, for you have one istructor, the Messiah. The greatest among you will be your servant. All who exalt themselves will be humbled, and all who humble themselves will be exalted."

MATTHEW 23:1-12

Some years ago friends and I went to hear the celebrated McGuire Sisters in concert. A large, enthusiastic crowd was present. Many of us had listened to the recordings of the famous sisters but had never seen them in person. Toward the end of their concert, we were a bit surprised to hear them sing a familiar gospel hymn. At first it seemed strangely out of place in the middle of all the popular songs they had sung. Then they explained that their mother had told them they should always include a hymn. Across the years, that hymn was a sturdy reminder that their now eminently successful singing career had begun in a tiny church in Ohio.

Humility, remembering our origins and all that we hold in common, is a most attractive virtue.

It was Oswald Chambers who said that the chief characteristic of a Christian is humility. When Jesus found that characteristic conspicuously absent in the lives of the religious leaders of his time, he ruthlessly exposed its absence.

Humility Is Being Equal with Others

The twenty-third chapter of Matthew is almost harsh in its tone. Jesus began by addressing the Pharisees and scribes, saying, "You love to sit on Moses' seat." Moses' seat may have been a piece of furniture in the synagogue, or it may have been a figurative expression for those who have the authority or the responsibility of presenting the Mosaic law. At any rate, those charged with the responsibility, at least those to whom Jesus spoke that day, did not shrink from that weighty responsibility but embraced it eagerly, indeed, competed for it. Jesus said, "You love to sit on that seat."

Then he said to the crowd, "Observe and do what they teach you, but do not do what they do. They preach but they do not practice." Indeed, they loaded the people down with heavy burdens; they gave them rules and regulations but didn't lift a finger to help them. Over against that is the claim of Jesus who told the people earlier, "My yoke is easy, and my burden is light" (Matt. 11:30).

Jesus then began in earnest to describe a religion that was essentially an external phenomenon. He wasn't so much criticizing individuals as he was criticizing an entire system of thought that would reduce a great religion to a matter of rules and regulations instead of a great, compelling affection and love for God. He said of the scribes and Pharisees, "You do your good deeds to be seen by people, not out of a love for God but to get the recognition of people." In another place, he talked about their long, pretentious prayers. He talked about all the things they did to be seen, and each time he said, "They have their reward." In other words, their only reward is being seen, and of what importance is that?

Jesus continued by saying, "You make your phylacteries broad and your fringes long." In the Old Testament, the Jewish people were told to take little leather pouches and bind them to their foreheads and to their left arms. In those pouches they had tiny scrolls with verses of scripture from Exodus and Deuteronomy. But, in order to make their piety more apparent, some people used very wide straps so that they caught the attention of all. They also made their fringes long.

The concept of the fringe is very interesting. In the book of Numbers, the Jews were told to put tassels on the four corners of their outer garments. In those tassels they were to include at least one strand of dyed royal blue thread. That is where we get the phrase *royal blue*. It was to be a reminder of who they were, the people of God. They had to get blue dye at great trouble and expense. It came only from the Murex snail, and they could extract only tiny quantities from each snail. The whole idea of the fringes and blue strands was a wonderful symbol and a reminder, but there was no stipulation on how long those fringes were to be. Jesus was talking about a group of people who made the fringes really long so that everyone who saw them enter the Temple with those tassels dragging the floor must have thought, "Oh, how holy these people are." In reality, Jesus was saying that they were anything but holy because their pride was literally eating up whatever religious devotion they may have had.

Jesus continued, "Oh, you love those salutations in the marketplace. You like to sit in the places of honor." Jesus told them that it would be much better to go to the foot of the table and be asked to come up than to start out at the head of the table and be asked to go down. That would be very embarrassing.

Jesus also chided the religious leaders about their love of being called *rabbi*. They were only beginning to use that term meaning teacher or great one. Jesus said, "You love to hear people call you 'teacher' or 'old great one,' but you only have one teacher, the Lord, and you only have one master, the Christ." Jesus was taking away these distinctions, these salutations that they liked.

Jesus was saying there is a radical equality among his people, and we are not to use terms to elevate one above the other.

But it is human, isn't it, to want to be a little bit higher than the rank and file? I remember the first conference I attended after I had received my doctorate. I was yearning for a way to make my distinction known. Nearby was a screen on which messages were left for people who had an emergency call or something of that kind. I sat there all week hoping my name would appear. Finally, just before the end of the week, they put my name, complete with my new title, on the screen. Wow! That was a fulfilling moment. It takes a while to realize that things we once thought were so great are similar to potato chips—they look bigger than they really are. Once you get the thing and close down on it, it doesn't amount to very much.

Jesus is saying to his followers, "You just don't need that. Let go of all that separates you." Of course, it is human to want to be important, and we all need a good ego and healthy self-esteem. But Jesus is saying, "Watch how you get these things." We have a lot of ways of boosting our ego and self-esteem in our culture, don't we?

I was visiting with someone not long ago, and the whole time I was there I heard background music that I hadn't heard before. I asked him about the music, and he said, "That is not ordinary music. Maybe it sounds ordinary to you, but there are subliminal messages in that music." I said, "Really? What is this tape we are listening to now? What is the message?" He said, "All through it there are these words: *You are okay. You are wonderful. You are great, and you are getting better every day. This is going to be the greatest day you've ever had.*"

He told me that he had been listening to the tape and that he was growing every day, getting more prominent and more important. Then I asked him how much it cost. His answer was depressing; people are willing to pay a lot of money to feel important. I guess the most depressing thing is that this was only a tape of someone else's voice, when in reality the real advance comes with a relationship to Almighty God.

Humility Is Serving Others

Jesus made a statement that became a proverb. Often on his lips, in his speeches, and in his sermons Jesus said, "Those who exalt themselves are going to be humbled, and those who humble themselves are going to be exalted. If you want to be great, you must be a servant." He also said, "I came into the world to serve; I did not come to be served."

Once when Jesus' disciples were too eaten up with pride to do it, he took a bowl and a towel and knelt and washed the dirty feet of his disciples, even the ones who betrayed him and the ones who ran away and deserted him. Jesus was a servant. Nobody ever was as humble as Jesus.

The Bible says that Jesus was lowly in heart and was willing to leave his throne in glory to take the robe of human flesh. He humbled himself and became obedient unto death, even to death on the cross. What happened when he humbled himself like that? The Bible says, "Therefore God also highly exalted him and gave him the name that is above every name" (Phil. 2:9). If you are looking for a classic definition of humility, it is "to have in our persons the spirit of Jesus Christ."

Humility goes beyond words. Jesus said he was lowly in heart, and we believe him. If others tell us they are humble, the hairs stand up on the backs of our necks. They are telling more about themselves than they really want to reveal.

I recall a certain professor who was always talking about his humility. One day when we were going out of his class, a friend said, "He is going to write another book; I can see it coming. This one will be entitled *Humility and How I Achieved It.*"

Evangelist Dwight L. Moody said, "That person who is marked by humility has achievements to be sure, but that person sees achievements in the light of God's power and not his own." There is a big difference.

Humility Is a By-product of Grace

You don't go out and get humility. You don't approach something with the attitude of "If I humble myself, I will be exalted." Achieving humility is not a technique; it is a way of life. Humility is a by-product—the by-product of having been brought into the presence of God, having come so fully into the presence of God that you become like Moses, who took off his shoes because he knew that common dirt was now holy ground. That is the beginning of humility.

Someone once said that humility is the first test of a Christian. If we pass the test of humility, we possess a curious feeling that lets us know that the greatness is not in ourselves but comes through us. It has its origins in another.

David Livingston, the great missionary physician, confessed that his life was not of any use to God until he reached the understanding that God had not intended him to be a great person. When he fought and won that battle, God began to use him. Of course, he *was* a great man, but he lost his life; and in losing it and laying it down, he found it.

Humility goes beyond words. When you are with someone who is marked by humility, you sense a quality of being at ease. You have a marvelous sense of being comfortable, because that person is not impressed with his or her greatness.

When I was a student in seminary, I once was asked if I would go pick up someone at the airport. When I was told who it was, I jumped at the chance. Wallace Hamilton was coming to preach at our seminary, and I had the opportunity to go meet him. Wallace Hamilton never attended seminary; he was educated in the University of Life and through the discipline of his own studies. What a remarkable preacher of the gospel! Every aspiring preacher wanted to sound just like Wallace Hamilton. Now I had the chance to go meet him and bring him back to the campus. I was in awe, but he didn't let me stay in awe very long. By the time we got back to the campus, it was as though we had been friends for a long time. He was not impressed with his own greatness.

Later I read the words of Andrew Murray, the devotional writer: "Humility is a perfect quietness in the heart." Then I understood what it was about Wallace Hamilton that I admired so much. He had a perfect quietness in his heart. He was not a noisy person, laying claim to all kinds of things for himself.

Every great person is marked by humility. It comes from knowing who you are, from having stood in the presence of Almighty God and being reminded of who you are, apart from him.

I once heard a story about Thomas Shepherd, the founder of Harvard University. Not many months before he died at age forty-four, someone found him one day lying on the floor of his office, face down, with the *New England Gazette* crumpled in his hand. He had crumpled that paper in his hand because he had published a sermon in that newspaper, and right beside his sermon was a more eloquent sermon. Shepherd could not stand to read it. He was holding that crumpled-up newspaper, lying on his face.

After Shepherd died, someone read in his journal that he had gone on a personal fast as a result of that experience. He fasted because he wanted to see the glory of Jesus Christ. He had never really seen that glory. And he wanted to let God help him with pride, the unhealthy pride remaining in his heart.

When we have been in God's presence, when we have experienced his life-transforming grace, then we live our lives in his glory. The apostle Paul kept saying it in his letter to the Ephesians. We live to "the praise of his glory." That is our calling and that is our destiny. Our testimony can be expressed by these words from the hymn "Amazing Grace": "Tis grace hath brought us safe thus far, And grace will lead us home."

I have heard many stories about Booker T. Washington. One story relates an event that led to Washington's selection as president of Tuskegee Normal School, forerunner of Tuskegee Institute. Washington was waiting to be interviewed by the selection committee, which preferred a white candidate. Knowing that his wait would be a long one because the other candidates were being interviewed first, Washington asked what he could do while he waited. Looking around at the untidy room in which they were standing, one committee member is said to have replied, "Why don't you clean up the room." Washington promptly took off his coat and carefully swept the room. Then he washed down the floor and the baseboards. Washington became the new president. The committee had been searching for one who, in addition to other qualifications, possessed the humility that would allow him to perform a common task.

Jack London's book *The Call of the Wild* is a classic. I think my son John must have read it a half-dozen times. We both liked reading the story about Buck, the big dog that lived in California but was stolen and made a sled dog in the frozen northlands, the wastelands of Alaska or beyond. If you have read it, you know that Buck was a cross between a St. Bernard and a German Shepherd, so he was really a strong, husky dog. The man who stole him while he was still a young dog was extremely brutal. Trying to break his spirit, the man clubbed, starved, and beat the dog. As you got caught up in the novel, you thought, "Well, the dog is going to die."

But just in time that broken, wounded, hurting animal came into the hands of John Thornton, a kind, loving man who cared tenderly for his animals. He nursed Buck back to health. There developed between John Thornton and that sled dog, Buck, a wonderful bond.

One day John Thornton went into a saloon. He had been out in the wilds a long time, and he went in there and drank too much. He started to wager on the strength of Buck, who was pretty well-known by this time. He made an outlandish claim that Buck was strong enough, even if hitched to a sled alone, to break a sled free of ice and drag it down the street loaded with one thousand pounds. Some may have tried that with three or four hundred pounds, but none would have tried it with one thousand pounds.

After the bets were made, they went to the street, and John Thornton hooked Buck to the sled. A few minutes later, he knelt and whispered something in the great dog's ear. Buck stood up and went first to the right and then to the left, and then, with all of his power, he jumped into the harness and broke that sled free. While the crowds stood and cheered, Buck dragged that sled down the street. Do you know what John Thornton whispered to Buck as he held his shaggy head? "As you love me, Buck, as you love me." That explained it.

When you see someone's life full of grace and humility, you can explain that, too, by a loving Lord who has healed a broken, wounded spirit, who has delivered our feet from falling and our eyes from tears. And the Master says to us as we stand before the test of life, "As you love me, as you love me." When we live to the praise of his glory, our lives will be marked with the grace of humility.

7.

With Obedience

Now by this we may be sure that we know him, if we obey his commandments. Whoever says, "I have come to know him," but does not obey his commandments, is a liar, and in such a person the truth does not exist; but whoever obeys his word, truly in this person the love of God has reached perfection. By this we may be sure that we are in him: whoever says, "I abide in him," ought to walk just as he walked.

Beloved, I am writing you no new commandment, but an old commandment that you have had from the beginning; the old commandment is the word that you have heard. 1 JOHN 2:3-7

I was standing in front of my hotel, suitcase in hand, waiting on a secretary whom I had never seen to drive me to the airport. After about five minutes, a woman in a station wagon drove up and, upon seeing me waiting, said, "Throw your suitcase in the back; we're on our way." I did as she directed and sat down on the front seat beside her. After about five minutes, I noticed that we were not going in the general direction of the airport. I asked her if she were taking a new route to the airport. "Airport!" she exclaimed, "You aren't Dr. Jones?" When I told her who I was, she slammed on the brakes, made a U-turn, and took me back to the hotel.

Life doesn't go very well for us when we just accept any invitation. In order to reach our destination in this life, we must heed one voice above all others; we must learn to obey God.

In the First Letter of John, the apostle John no longer resembles that firebrand who once said to Jesus, "Lord, those people don't want to have anything to do with you, so bring down fire upon them." Indeed, he has long since become the apostle of love. His letter sounds like that of an aged pastor, a spiritual father, for he addresses the people in his church as "my little children," or he calls them "beloved." There is an affectionate tenderness in all that he says.

In all of John's letters, and especially this first one, John poses some tests concerning the ethical dimension of our faith. He is responding to some false teachers who had infiltrated the church. The people were confused, and John is giving them some simple tests by which they can know if they are walking in the light, if they have fellowship with God and love one another. If they are honest, if they have stopped deceiving themselves and have begun to believe that they have indeed committed sin, these tests will show it.

Obedience Is a Test of Faith

In I John 2:3, John poses a test concerning those who claim to know God. He says, "By this we may be sure." Isn't that positive language? "Now by this we may be sure that we know him, if we obey his commandments." Then in the fourth verse, he goes on to say that if someone says, "I know him," but disobeys his commandments, then that person is a liar. What becomes of all that tenderness? How is it that suddenly there is such a shift as that? He does not say that if someone says, "I know him," but deliberately disobeys his commandments, then that person has a momentary lapse and is a little bit confused, needs a little bit more clarity. He says that if a person does that, then that individual is a liar. From someone who has just been talking about "his little children," that comes across with a jarring kind of reality.

What John is saying is that obedience has always been the test of our faith. We are perfected as we keep God's word. We are perfected as we walk as he walked, as we imitate Christ. And, of course, the whole of scripture backs John up in this. James said it so bluntly, "So faith by itself, if it has no works, is dead" (James 2:17). And then Paul said in speaking to Titus that those who profess to know Christ deny him by their deeds. Paul said that their very consciences have been corrupted. He said that they can no longer trust their consciences to guide them because they have professed one thing but have done another. Now it was to people like this that John was speaking when he said that someone who claims to know God but does not keep his commandments does not have the truth in him.

Jesus also insisted on obedience. He once told the story about a man who had two sons. The father went to the first son and said, "Son, go and work in my vineyard today." Shame on the son for having to be asked! Everyone knows God wants us to work in his vineyard, to do the very things that Jesus did while he was on this earth. But the father did ask him, and that son respectfully said, "I will, sir." But he did not go. The father went to the second son and asked, "Son, would you go and work in my vineyard today?" This Son was rude and disrespectful to his father. He said, "I will not." But afterward, he repented and went. And Jesus said, "Which of these two sons did the will of the father?" They answered rightly, saying, "Well, the second." Jesus said, "That is correct." Repentance leads the way to obedience, and obedience is what Christ requires of all of us who would know him—*really* know him.

Obedience Leads to Spiritual Growth

Tennyson said, "Our wills are ours, we know not how; Our wills are ours, to make them thine." To make our wills God's will is not easy. Oswald Chambers said that the golden rule of spiritual growth is obedience. He said if you want scientific information, the key to acquiring it is intellectual curiosity; but if you want insight into the nature and the person of Jesus Christ, the key to that insight is obedience. There is no other way.

Through obedience we grow in our understanding of God and of who we are. If we are in intellectual darkness, it is because of ignorance. If we are in spiritual darkness, it is because of disobedience. If our faith has grown cold, if our experiences have become stale, if prayer has become perfunctory and church work has become meaningless and worship has lost its thrill and excitement, then we must begin to examine our lives to see at which point we first began to disobey our God. Growth in Jesus Christ continues only as we obey.

There was a time in my own life when the Lord made my call as plain to me as could be made, and yet I did not yield. I attended a Call to Preach Conference at a distant university to explore all the implications of going into the ministry. I did not go to that Call to Preach Conference because I wanted to know more about the ministry. I went to get some ammunition so I could argue with God about why I didn't want to be a preacher. I wanted to sit down and unravel that call by talking about what this means and what that means and what this implication is and what that implication is, when, in reality, the only way to grow in my understanding of Christ would have been through obedience.

I remember reading how General Montgomery went to North Africa to take command when the Allied forces were in disarray. Shortly after he arrived, he found out why the army was floundering. The officers were taking their orders so lightly that they were not orders at all. General Montgomery called all of his subordinates together and told them that orders are for acting upon, not for the basis of discussion. When we get that straight, things begin to turn around and things begin to happen. When our Lord calls us to do something or to be something, when he puts something on our hearts, he expects us to use that as a basis for action, not as a source of conversation, argument, or armchair quarterbacking.

Peter Marshall once preached a sermon called "Under Sealed Orders." He was referring to the times when the captain of an ocean-going vessel would be given orders and would be told by his commander that he was not to open those orders until he was out to sea; it was only after he had gone out to sea that he opened the orders and learned the ship's destination.

Christians experience the same thing. We are under sealed orders. We do not begin to understand what the next step is, or where the Lord is leading us, until we first agree to go out to sea. Some of us stay in port and wonder why our experience has grown cold.

Some of us are like Moses when he was trapped between Pharaoh's army and the Red Sea. Moses saw Pharaoh's army closing in behind him, and the people panicked. Moses held up his hands for quiet and said, "Listen, stand still and watch the Lord fight for you." And in the face of that, God thundered at Moses from the heavens saying, "Why do you stand there saying, 'Watch the Lord fight for you'? You speak to the people that they move forward." And when Moses spoke to the people and they moved forward, the path was opened before them, and they went across on dry land.

In ancient times people carried their lamps not in their hands but in the toes of their shoes. These primitive lamps would shine three feet out in front of their wearers. A person could take one secure step and see to take another step and another step and another. Even so, we grow in our understanding of Jesus Christ.

You may be very sure that you know Christ if you are obeying him in the smallest details. Only as we obey in those smallest details do the larger responsibilities become plain. We grow as we obey.

Obedience Is a Joyful Response

Some might say that our salvation is contingent on what we do. Not at all! In our Christian understanding, faith is the foundation of all that we do, including our good works. Before he was converted, Paul obeyed God in order to be saved. After he was converted, he obeyed God only because he was saved. That is the great difference between salvation by works and salvation by faith. Faith is a personal relationship with Jesus Christ that becomes the foundation of all our works.

Think about that struggle I had with God's call for my life. It was not just a call to the ministry; it was a call to become a Christian. All the while God was calling me, I was determined to show him that I wasn't really Christian material. I went through a very rebellious time and did things that would cause shame for almost anybody. I remember thinking that surely now God is going to let me alone—that voice and that yearning that keep pulling at me are somehow going to be still, and he will let me go my own way. But in the face of my rebellion, I kept encountering a love that was not contingent on how I behaved. I kept experiencing grace even as I stood in the middle of the prison of sin that I had built around myself. I continued to realize, though, that God loved me in spite of what I was doing and in spite of who I was. Christ was revealed to me in a very special experience, and after that experience, I summed it up the next morning, saying, "If you can love me like that, knowing all that I am, then the least I can do is to spend the rest of my life serving you."

When we see Christ, we instantly obey him. When we have a vision of Christ on the cross and of his love for us, then instantly we want to lay down our lives for him. That is the way we are sure we know him. It's like a letter a woman sent me whose heart is running over with love because Christ has filled her life. She wrote, "How can I give more of myself back to him?" It is like a lay pastor who said after his conversion, "I gave my soul; I gave my life; I gave my possessions; and I grieved because there was no more to give."

Some might argue that such obedience is difficult, but Jesus' burden is light and his yoke is easy. When Jesus calls us to do a work for him, it is because he has done a work of faith and love in us that makes our obedience a joy. If it is not a joy, then we need to examine ourselves.

Someone is reported to have asked Emily Post, the etiquette expert, how to respond to an invitation to attend a function at the White House to be held on the same evening as another important engagement. The inquirer wanted to be appropriate in expressing his regrets. Emily Post said that there are no proper regrets for an invitation to the White House. Such an invitation takes precedence over all others. In the same manner, a Christian must obey the call of Christ above every other summons.

Stonewall Jackson's biography tells how one day he was at his camp, which was miles from that of General Robert E. Lee, when he learned from a messenger that the general wished to see him. In that message the general said, "It is not a matter of any great importance, so come at your leisure." Jackson had his horse saddled and immediately set out to the general's camp. The amazing thing was that it was in the middle of the worst storm they had had for a long time. It was sleeting, and the road was mud and ice. Jackson got to the general's camp just as the general was finishing breakfast. Lee looked out of his tent and saw Jackson riding through the sleet and the snow. As he rushed out to Jackson, he said, "Man, I told you it was not a matter of great importance." Jackson said, "When my general wishes to see me, my general's wish is my command."

Do we feel that way about Jesus? Is the wish of Jesus our command? By this you can be sure you know him if you keep his commandments.

A translator working on the Wycliffe Bible was having a difficult time translating the New Testament into a native dialect. He was particularly stumped by the word *obedience*. There was no native word for *obedience*. He struggled and struggled, but he simply could not find the word. One day he was going back to the compound where he lived, and while he was yet some distance, he whistled for his dog. The dog, hearing his master's whistle, jumped to his feet and ran and jumped into the arms of his master. One of the natives standing by who saw that dog said, "The missionary's dog was all ears." The missionary said, "That is my word," and he took that word and put it in the New Testament for the word *obedience*. The obedient Christian is "all ears."

Like Samuel, when the Lord calls our name, we say, "Here am I, Lord," and like Isaiah, "Here am I, send me." And we go from strength to strength in our obedience until finally, like that devout man of old, we can say, "I delight, O God, I delight to do thy will."

8.

With Voluntary Suffering

Beloved, do not be surprised at the fiery ordeal that is taking place among you to test you, as though something strange were happening to you. But rejoice insofar as you are sharing Christ's sufferings, so that you may also be glad and shout for joy when his glory is revealed. If you are reviled for the name of Christ, you are blessed, because the spirit of glory, which is the Spirit of God, is resting on you. But let none of you suffer as a murderer, a thief, a criminal, or even as a mischief maker. Yet if any of you suffers as a Christian, do not consider it a disgrace, but glorify God because you bear this name. For the time has come for judgment to begin with the household of God; if it begins with us, what will be the end for those who do not obey the gospel of God?
And
"If it is hard for the righteous to be saved,
what will become of the ungodly and the sinners?"
Therefore, let those suffering in accordance with God's will entrust themselves to a faithful Creator, while continuing to do good.

1 PETER 4:12-19

I have almost been haunted by one line that was a part of a television documentary on human suffering. The documentary, shown some years ago, was a discussion of how medical science has alleviated so much human suffering. As I watched the program, I applauded almost every single part of it. But the last line in this documentary bothered me. The commentator said, "Americans agree on one thing. Suffering is not good for anyone, certainly not for them."

It then struck me that Jesus of Nazareth was out of step with prevailing attitudes because it was he who said, "Blessed (or happy) are those who are persecuted for my sake, who are spoken evil of and otherwise treated badly on my account, because their reward is great in heaven." A Savior who could say that has to be out of step with what most Americans feel about suffering. One thing is for sure: we have to be prepared to respond to suffering because suffering is at the core of human existence.

Our Response to Suffering

It is true that sometimes we need to side-step suffering, rather than embrace it as our Savior apparently did. We need to make sure we don't bring on our own suffering. The Bible says we should never suffer as a murderer, as a thief, as a wrongdoer, or as a mischief maker. While not many of us have suffered for being a murderer or a thief, some of us would be guilty of being a mischief maker and a wrongdoer. What is our trespass? Are we pessimistic or optimistic toward suffering?

In the Middle Ages, the response to suffering was pessimistic. Most of the people in the Middle Ages believed that the suffering they endured throughout all of life on this earth was somehow a repayment for sins that their forebears had committed. When they spoke of their forebears, they went all the way back to Adam and Eve. It was a very fat contract, and it could easily explain away all of the suffering that anyone endures in this world.

We take another approach to the whole idea of suffering. We are addicted to ease and comfort. We somehow have adopted the attitude that life owes us at least eighty or eighty-five years of painless bliss. If anything comes along to interrupt that bliss, we are apt to react in a very destructive way, with anger and bitterness.

When suffering impinges upon us, some of us are apt to give up or to give in and seek solace in alcohol or drugs. Alcohol and drugs can desensitize us to the pain and enable us to ignore the problems creating the pain. M. Scott Peck, in his well-known book *The Road Less Traveled*, said that the primary basis for human mental illness lies in our attempt to avoid suffering. Carl Jung put it even more dramatically when he said that neurosis is a substitute for legitimate suffering.

In our day, suffering is out. It is a bad word. It is depressing even to mention it. We are so desperate to avoid suffering of any kind that if a tragic reality confronts us that we cannot escape, if problems are there that seem insurmountable, then we give up. It is becoming more and more commonplace in this society for people to take their own lives. They have forgotten the promises of God, or they fly in the face of God's promises and persuade themselves that by ending their lives, all possibilities for suffering are also ended. So, they end their lives rather than embrace the harsh realities and continue to live lives that, of necessity, include suffering.

For many, faith and suffering are simply contradictory. How can you even speak of them in the same breath, let alone in the same conversation? In the book *After Auschwitz*, the author, Richard Rubenstein, wonders how anyone could, after seeing Hitler's death camps, continue to believe in a loving God who acts lovingly toward his children. He says that it is ridiculous, after seeing those death camps, to believe in a loving God. How many times have you heard people say, "I can't believe in a God who permits suffering like that"? You see, with the encroachment of suffering, we reject God.

There are some people who go to the other end of the spectrum. Instead of rejecting God when they suffer, they serve God and reject suffering. They have a theology that says that if you believe right, if you say all the right things and push all the right faith buttons, then you need never suffer again. Not only will you be free of pain, but you also will be wealthy and healthy. So there is one reaction that says because I suffer, I reject God, and another reaction that says because I have God, I reject suffering. One is as superficial and insufficient as the other.

Harold Kushner's best-selling book *When Bad Things Happen to Good People* was the subject of a recent magazine article. The article concluded that the book's popularity stems not only from the fact that it is well-written, but also from the fact that it relates to a narcissistic age like ours, an age that basically believes all suffering is unfair and undeserved.

The Cost of Christianity

How easily we accept the designation "good" for ourselves, whereas Jesus applied it only to God. We grab onto it so quickly for ourselves, applying it to almost anyone who pays his or her taxes and doesn't abuse the family. It is no longer fashionable in this age to trust a faithful Creator who is able to help us bear our sufferings and face our tragedies. That is no longer a popular message. But in the face of our culture, a text comes to us saying, "Do not be surprised by this fiery trial. Do not be shocked or surprised by what you are to suffer." Why shouldn't we be surprised? Why shouldn't we be shocked when we are called upon to suffer? Because Jesus suffered. Start right there. Jesus suffered, and the cross is a symbol of our faith. Jesus suffered, and the servant is not above the master.

Hoffman said, "It would be arrogant for Christians to somehow believe that God should give us a life different from the life he gave his only Son." Think about that for a moment. We are different from the world. We are different from non-Christians. We have one overriding consideration that guides and directs everything we do. This text from 1 Peter says that we were guided by our flesh and our bodily appetites, but now we are guided by God's Spirit.

No wonder we have difficulty in the world. Our friends are surprised that we no longer engage in carousing and drunkenness and reveling and unbridled immorality. They are surprised that we no longer do those things, and they sometimes chide us because we no longer join them. The abuse may take the shape of nicknames or teasing or whatever; it is there nonetheless.

If all of those who went before us suffered, why, then, should we expect a painless existence as followers of Christ? John Wesley said if he went three days without someone throwing an egg or a brick at him, or saying an ugly word to him, he would get on his knees and ask God if he had fallen short. If we feel totally at home in our world, it says something about us.

Does it pay to be a Christian in our culture? There was a time when it paid. Does it still pay? I saw an auto repair shop several years ago with a big sign out in front that said, "If you will bring a bulletin from your church when you come, we will give you a $2 discount on your repair bill." I thought, *Well, it does pay, but it doesn't pay very much!* The truth is, it costs something to be a Christian.

One day I had breakfast with a man who had a very prosperous business. Something wonderful had happened to that man; he had been converted in a recent service of worship. He came to me as his pastor and said, "Because I have accepted Christ as my personal Savior, I don't feel comfortable with some of the things I have been doing in my business."

I said, "Tell me about your situation." He said, "I have been engaged in price-fixing with some of my supposed competitors. There has been collusion. We have been setting the bids; we have been rigging the bid, and we have been taking turns. We have been putting our competitors out of business by keeping them from getting the big jobs."

He then said, "Now that I am a Christian, I cannot do that anymore, and I have told them I can't do it. They say that if I squeal, they will get the law on me because they have proof of my past involvement. They tell me that if I drop out, they will put me out of business, too."

He didn't go along with them, and they did put him out of business. He couldn't go along with the system, and he went broke. It costs something to be a Christian.

Isaac Watts said, "Is this vile world a friend to grace, to help me on to God?" I don't think so. My reading and my observations just don't lead me to the conclusion that this world is a friend to God. Why then, since we belong to the commonwealth of heaven, should we be surprised at these fiery trials that confront us? The Scriptures say we are to rejoice in our suffering. We are to rejoice because we are with Christ, because Christ himself suffered, and, as Paul said, "We would do anything to share in the fellowship of that suffering."

Christians Choose Suffering

The early church said that suffering is a gift, for it has been given to us not only to believe in his name, but also to suffer for him. There is a kinship in that suffering, and we know that God understands. God put this nervous system of ours together, so God knows about all our suffering. But God never suffered physical pain until he came in the person of Jesus. As someone has said, "Jesus is the only person in the world who bears his scars in heaven. Jesus is the only one in heaven who has any scars." Why did Jesus take those scars even in his glorified body? He took those scars as an eternal reminder of the reality of suffering.

But what we are talking about here is not involuntary suffering. We are talking about voluntary suffering. No one made Jesus bear that cross. He did it out of loyalty to a higher purpose. I hear people saying, "This is my cross to bear," and they talk about something that has been imposed upon them. But anything that is involuntarily thrust upon us is not a cross to bear. That is not voluntary suffering. Jesus invites us to take up our cross and follow him. When we willingly subscribe to a higher loyalty, to a supreme allegiance that requires suffering of us and from us, that is voluntary suffering. When we suffer like that, we share a kinship with Jesus Christ that is absolutely remarkable. The amazing thing is that when we know him in the fellowship of his suffering, having committed ourselves to a high and a holy purpose that necessitates suffering in this world, it begins to color everything, including the involuntary suffering that comes upon us.

My grandfather was a devout Christian. In his later years he developed skin cancer on his face. The medical treatment available to him at that time was inadequate. In a few months, the cancer had progressed to the point that my grandfather was in constant pain. His great discomfort was apparent to me even though I was a small boy. Still, my grandfather never compained but endured his suffering.

One day I asked Grandfather how he could stand the pain. His response was, "Jesus has suffered much more than this for me. I know he understands, and he will help me bear it."

What about you? Can you trust your soul to a faithful creator? The hymn "The Way of the Cross Leads Home" says it well: "I shall ne'er get sight of the Gates of Light, If the way of the cross I miss."

9.

With Kindness

If we live by the Spirit, let us also be guided by the Spirit. Let us not become conceited, competing against one another, envying one another.

My friends, if anyone is detected in a transgression, you who have received the Spirit should restore such a one in a spirit of gentleness. Take care that you yourselves are not tempted. Bear one another's burdens, and in this way you will fulfill the law of Christ.

Do not be deceived; God is not mocked, for you reap whatever you sow. If you sow to your own flesh, you will reap corruption from the flesh; but if you sow to the Spirit, you will reap eternal life from the Spirit. So let us not grow weary in doing what is right, for we will reap at harvest-time, if we do not give up. So then, whenever we have an opportunity, let us work for the good of all, and especially for those of the family of faith.

GALATIANS 5:25-6:2, 7-10

Kindness Is a Challenge in a Toughened World

In our culture, kindness is a challenge. Sometimes it is difficult to be kind even in the closest circles, even in our families. In one of the "Family Circle" comic strips, the little girl had broken something of value. Her mother heard the crash that resounded through the house. The mother stood over her daughter with a threatening look, opened her mouth, and was about to say something when the little girl interrupted and said, "Mother, whatever you are going to say now, please say it in your telephone voice." It is not easy, even in our families, to keep our telephone voices, and that is such a simple courtesy.

The fact that it is difficult to be kind in our families is brought home to us in some of the most dramatic ways we can imagine. Each time I see new evidence of child abuse in our culture, I am appalled. It is hard to understand how we could brutalize our young.

One day a young woman came to me with a look of indictment on her face. She reminded me of how she acted when she was a teenager in one of the churches I served. She asked, "Didn't you think my behavior was bizarre?" I said, "Well, yes, I thought you acted a little strange at times." She then said, "Didn't you ever wonder what was behind that behavior?" Truthfully, I had not. She said, "You mean all those years you did not suspect that my father, my own father, was sexually abusing me?" I stood there trying to comprehend her pain and realizing how oblivious I had been to it.

If ever we are going to end the horrible problem of child abuse, then we must first open our eyes to its reality. Then we can begin to ask ourselves what we must do to create families and communities so that this kind of thing does not happen.

We are also seeing brutality in our families these days in response to young men and women who have AIDS. It is appalling, but again and again I talk with someone who has been driven from home and kindred to die alone in a strange city at a time when a person needs a family network desperately. They need that "anyhow kind of love" that God has for all his people. Families are supposed to give that kind of love at a time when it is needed most. I cannot begin to understand how a father or a mother can say to a son or a daughter, "You must get out of this house; I never want to see you again." How did we become that brutal?

How have we reached this place in our culture? Is it because our children sit an average of three and a half hours every day in front of the television? Is it because, in many homes, children have the privilege of indiscriminately viewing any kind of program they wish to view? As our children look at the programs that are served up to their young minds, is this the trashing of our traditional values, norms, and ethics? They see the most grotesque, the most bizarre kinds of programs, all of them offered in the name of reality. Any time there is an outcry, the response is, "That is the way the real world is." The networks show it in the name of reality. When are we going to say to the sponsors who pay for those programs, "Enough of your reality!"

Is our toughening and our emotional callousness a kind of self-defense because we are constantly being bombarded with bad news and horrible happenings? When something awful happens—whether it is next door or across the world—in a matter of minutes we know about it; it is brought into our living rooms. Have we become so toughened because of our self-defense mechanism that we shrug off the hurts of others? And once we get that toughened, do we then begin to shrug off the hurts of those who are our neighbors and our friends and even our family?

When I was a boy, we were allowed to take off our shoes in the springtime of the year. It was the bare-foot season. When we first took our shoes off, we would cringe and limp around the house. Every little twig or pebble hurt our feet. As the summer wore on, though, we could run over anything. Those feet got tough.

Has that happened to our sensitivities and our emotions? Have we just become tough, so that we accept the brutality of the system? We have been called to be like God. That is the meaning behind the teaching of Jesus when he said, "You are to be like God, who is kind to the ungrateful and even to the selfish."

How can Christians have a tit-for-tat mentality? Even the non-believers do good to those who do good to them, and even the non-believers forgive those who forgive them. Why, even sinners do that. Jesus said that is an ordinary ethic. Anyone can return a favor. Jesus is talking about an extraordinary ethic. He is talking about loving your enemies and being kind to those who despitefully use you. We have a radical ethic to introduce to the world. Jesus says, "You are to be like God, who himself is kind."

Kindness Breaks Down Barriers

In the teachings of Jesus, we have a true portrait of God. Jesus states matter-of-factly that God is kind, and we are the sons and the daughters of the most high God, who is kind even to those who are ungrateful and selfish.

It is interesting that the word *kind* and the word *kin* come from the same Old English root word. We are supposed to be kind to those to whom we are kin. Then, when we are kind to strangers, somehow we feel kin to them and are drawn close to them. When we are kind people, we have a kinship with God. Jesus says we become like God in our kindness. Kindness breaks down all barriers between us and makes us real.

Recently I decided to take our grandchildren to the park. The schools were on holiday, but I was surprised to see so many people waiting to get on the children's train. I did not expect the park to be so crowded. I just knew that with all six of the grandchildren visiting, we had to do something.

At the little train station, you find a place to put your strollers, you open the gate for one another, and you do all of those neighborly kinds of things. The train cars are very small—they are made for children—but I had to carry the eight-month-old twins onto the train. I folded my body into one of those seats and held the babies on my knee because I could not get them on my lap. Then the train started making all sorts of frightening sounds. I worried about the little children being afraid, so I started making familiar clicking, clucking sounds that parents and grandparents make. I felt a little self-conscious, except that all around me everybody was whistling, clicking, clucking, cooing, and making those comforting sounds, too. Suddenly I felt very much at home with that entire trainload of people. We were all just alike.

Wouldn't it be wonderful if we could just set aside all of those stern, somber looks and the idea that "You have your problems but don't bother me; I don't want to hear it"? Wouldn't it be wonderful if all of us who can cluck and whistle with little children could just be that vulnerable all the time, in the places where we work and with all the people we meet? What has made the difference for us, anyway?

Kindness Begins with Kindness

Read the words of the hymn "Rescue the Perishing":

Down in the human heart, crushed by the tempter,
Feelings lie buried that grace can restore;
Touched by a loving heart, Wakened by kindness,
Chords that are broken will vibrate once more.

I believe we are awakened by kindness, not by a threat.

Augustine was one of the greatest Christians who ever lived, and he was converted by Ambrose. As Augustine talked about his conversion, he said he first began to love that man not only as a great teacher of truth but also as a person who was kind. Isn't that where we begin?

I remember the man who was my pastor at the church where I became a Christian and decided to go into the ministry. I do not recall very much about his sermons, but I do remember being moved by them. I remember liking the way he preached. But, most of all, I remember his kindness. When I was struggling with going into the ministry, he invited me to go to a preacher's conference. The first afternoon we were there, the conference went into a series of reports. That pastor looked at the seventeen-year-old beside him, nudged me with his elbow, and said, "Let's get out of here." So while the speaker was looking the other way, we got up and slipped out. He took me to a movie theater, and we saw a great Western. I thought, "This guy saved my life, because he knew I would have never gone into the ministry if I had had to sit through all of those reports." He always considered the thoughts and feelings of the people around him.

Some people say that Beethoven's "Moonlight Sonata" was his best composition. Through that sonata, he was trying to help a blind girl see moonlight on the water. That piece had its origin in an act of kindness. I believe that our path to Christ and the really good things in our lives has its origins in acts of kindness.

Kindness is part of who we are as Christians. We have looked into the face of a man who was crucified for us. We have looked into the face of Jesus, and when we looked into his eyes, we expected to find condemnation. We deserved condemnation, but when we looked into his eyes, we did not see condemnation. Instead, we found grace. That kindness changed everything for us.

A woman had broken the commandments, and she sat at the well talking with Jesus. After a time, she ran back to the village so excited that she forgot the water pot she had brought out to the well. She ran back shouting at the top of her voice, "Come see a man who told me everything I ever did!" But what excited that woman was not just that Jesus knew everything about her; he also wanted to give her living water. He offered her his friendship; he offered her his love; he offered her his forgiveness.

Kindness is what awakens us. Kindness is what brings us to inquire and to reach out after this same Jesus Christ. Kindness is one of those superb virtues that begets itself. Kindness begets kindness.

Some of the most dramatic instances of this truth are to be seen in a hospital. I have seen people go into the hospital and not even get settled in their rooms before they are bragging on their nurses. They will say, "Oh, you just ought to see my nurse! My nurse is so caring and so concerned about me." Every time you go to see people like that in the hospital, you have to push the nurses aside. The nurses congregate in those patients' rooms. They love to adjust their beds and fix their pillows and all the rest of it. However, when someone goes into the hospital who is angry and has a chip on his or her shoulder, that person can flash the call light all night long and the nurses will flip coins to see who has to answer it.

We also see kindness multiply in traffic. We've all experienced it. We're in a hurry, and we're trapped in traffic. Perhaps we're trapped on a side street, and we need to get onto a busy main street, but there is no traffic light. Some good Samaritan stops and lets us in, and we are so thankful for his or her kindness. Then we don't go thirty yards before somebody else tries to get out from another side street. We don't have time to stop; we're in a hurry. But we look in the mirror and see that good Samaritan, and we stop.

There is a story of a traveler going from city to city. He came to one city and asked, "What kind of people live here?" A very wise man at the city gate inquired of him, "What kind of people lived in the city where you once lived?" The traveler said, "Oh, they were mean and inconsiderate." The wise man replied, "Then you will find the people in this city mean and inconsiderate, too." The traveler went on to the next town and again inquired, "What kind of people live here?" The residents in the second town also asked him, "Well, what kind of people lived where you came from?" This time, he changed his story and answered, "Oh, they were wonderful and loving and kind." Warmly, the townsfolk responded, "Same kind of people live here."

When we begin to give kindness, we get kindness. It is one of those virtues that has its reward on earth. We don't have to wait until we get to heaven because we can be rewarded right here and now. Luke 6:38 tells us: "Give and it will be given to you. A good measure, pressed down, shaken together, running over, will be put into your lap."

Do you know what a lap is? I don't mean the narrow kind. I mean laps like my grandmother's. My grandmother always wore a great big cotton dress that went all the way down to her ankles, and she wore an apron on top of that dress. She would sit down in a rocking chair on the front porch and spread that lap. She could hold more butter beans on her lap than my brother and I could carry in a huge Number 3 washtub. Now that is a lap! When Jesus says, "I'll fill your lap," think about the kind of lap my grandmother had.

Called to Be Imitators of God

How do we make ourselves candidates for all of that kindness? We become candidates when we become kind ourselves. We are called to be imitators of God. Paul spells it out in Ephesians 4:32 when he says, "Be kind to one another, tenderhearted, forgiving one another, as God in Christ has forgiven you."

I saw an old friend of mine at a high school reunion. We were sitting down at the end of the table, terribly bored, while they went through the old routine of everybody standing up and saying how long they have been married and what great children they have. While we were waiting, my classmate went to get something to drink. While she was gone, the people at my end of the table started talking about her. "Did you see those shoes? Look at that handbag! What about those rings? Get a load of that dress! Isn't she uppity? Who does she think she is?" I went to join my friend, and we began to talk. She said, "Do you remember my husband?" I said, "I played beside him on our football team for four years; of course I remember him. Didn't you get married on graduation night?" She said, "Yes, we had been in love since junior high school. A few years ago, a hurricane drowned my husband."

While I was looking for words to say something kind to her about her husband, she said, "He didn't leave me alone; he left me a beautiful nineteen-year-old daughter. Soon after her father died, she went into her room, took out a gun that we didn't know she had, and killed herself." As I sat there trying to take all of that in and trying to find a word to say, I looked back at the table where we had come from, and I thought how often we fail to see the size of others' problems.

My friend had left the table because she couldn't brag about a husband she didn't have; she couldn't tell about a daughter who had taken her life. No wonder Ian MacLaren said that we should be kind because everyone is fighting a hard battle. Beneath that mask of courage lies a wounded, broken heart.

Be kind, and when you are kind, you will be like your Heavenly Father, who is kind even to the selfish and the ungrateful.

10.
With Confidence

What then are we to say about these things? If God is for us, who is against us? He who did not withhold his own Son, but gave him up for all of us, will he not with him also give us everything else? Who will bring any charge against God's elect? It is God who justifies. Who is to condemn? It is Christ Jesus, who died, yes, who was raised, who is at the right hand of God, who indeed intercedes for us. Who will separate us from the love of Christ? Will hardship, or distress, or persecution, or famine, or nakedness, or peril, or sword? As it is written,

> *"For your sake we are being killed all day long;*
> *we are accounted as sheep to be slaughtered."*

No, in all these things we are more than conquerors through him who loved us. For I am convinced that neither death, nor life, nor angels, nor rulers, nor things present, nor things to come, nor powers, nor height, nor depth, nor anything else in all creation, will be able to separate us from the love of God in Christ Jesus our Lord.

ROMANS 8:31-39

"What do you know?" is a common greeting in the area of the country in which I grew up. It is an open-ended question to which one may respond appropriately in almost any way. Carl Sandburg tells a story that has helped me understand that such a question is a very important one.

As the story goes, one day Sandburg was riding in the smoker car of a train. He liked riding in the smoker car because that is where the "deadheads" rode. The deadheads were those men who had finished their day's work on the railroad and were taking the train back to their home base. Sandburg loved observing the tired workers and listening to their conversations.

He records how one day he was sitting there in the smoker car when a fireman and a brakeman got onto the train and sat down in the seat in front of him. As the fireman slouched down into his seat, he posed a question to his brakeman friend. Without even looking at his friend, the fireman asked, "What do you know?" After a few seconds' pause, the fireman added, "For sure."

Sandburg thought it was a keen, intelligent question. All of us should raise it with ourselves. What do we know today for sure?

It is the legacy of a Christian to live this life with supreme confidence, no matter what the nature of our external lives and circumstances. The confidence I am describing is not the kind described in the self-help books that suggest one, two, three steps to build oneself up. There is some value in that kind of confidence, but the confidence I am describing cannot be found in a book or on a videotape in the rack beside the cash register at the check-out counter at your grocery store. The confidence I am describing is the heritage of every Christian. It goes beyond human understanding; it goes beyond the flesh itself. It is of God.

Confidence Is Knowing God Is for Us

The apostle Paul, writing to the Philippians long ago, stated something about his confidence in the flesh, his assurance concerning his own person. He said, "If anyone had a right to have confidence in the flesh, it was I, born of the tribe of Benjamin, a Hebrew of the Hebrews who had been circumcised on the eighth day, with everything done in accordance with the law."

Paul was a Pharisee, blameless in the keeping of the law and zealous in his actions. He persecuted those who transgressed the law. Paul had many reasons for confidence in the flesh. But then he said, "I regard everything as loss because of the surpassing value of knowing Christ Jesus my Lord" (Phil. 3:8*a*). Paul's confidence went beyond the flesh, beyond mere human understanding.

The origin of Paul's confidence is seen in the question he poses to the Romans: "What then are we to say about these things? If God is for us, who is against us?" (Rom. 8:31). In this scripture we have the words of life. This truth is an absolute for every Christian. It is not relative; it is not dependent upon the winds and trends of our time. It is as true now as it was two thousand years ago. Who can stand against us if God is for us?

There is a line in *The King and I* that says, in effect, "Sometimes I think I am not so sure of the things of which I am absolutely certain." If you think that is convoluted language, you are exactly right. It is very obscure. But sometimes we act as though we aren't sure about God being for us. Someone asked Robert Browning, "What is the one consistent thread or theme or conviction that goes through all of your writing?" Without hesitating at all, Browning responded, "I am very sure of God."

Do you have that confidence that comes from knowing God is for you? God is not against you. God is for you, and if he is for you, how can anything ultimately stand against you? "He who did not withhold his own Son, but gave him up for all of us, will he not with him also give us everything else?" (Rom. 8:32) Will a God who would not withhold his only Son not meet you with all the provisions of grace that you need during this life and in the world to come?

That verse may be old hat for some of us, but when Paul spoke it, the Jews in the crowd perked up their ears. Paul was essentially paraphrasing what God said to Abraham in the twenty-second chapter of Genesis. God tested the depths of Abraham's love and respect and obedience. God tested him by asking him to sacrifice his son Isaac, the son of the promise and the son of the covenant. In complete obedience, Abraham took Isaac and climbed Mount Moriah and was about to offer him as a sacrifice when God spoke to him and said, "Hold up. I know you would not withhold any of yourself; I know you respect me and love me and fear me. I know this because you would not withhold even your son but were willing to deliver him up."

This is the ultimate proof that God himself has justified us, forgiven us, because he put us right with himself at the expense of the death of his only Son, Jesus Christ. Now, who shall bring any charge against God's elect? Who is going to charge us if Almighty God himself has declared us pardoned, forgiven, redeemed, and put right with himself because of the death of Jesus Christ? Who is going to bring any charge against us? Who can make any kind of claim against us?

Harry Emerson Fosdick, while pastor at Riverside Church in New York City, often found himself counseling students from Columbia University. One afternoon he was talking with a young man who said he did not believe in God. Fosdick questioned him along these lines: "Well, then, how would you describe the God in whom you do not believe?" The young man described the God that he did not believe in, and when he finished, Fosdick said, "Well, young man, we are in the same boat. I don't believe in the God you've described, either."

If yours is a God who is out to get you, I don't believe in that God. If yours is a God who delights to judge his people and likes to put them down and make them feel ashamed and guilty, I don't believe in that God, either. I believe in a God who has forgiven us even at the cost of his own Son's life. We celebrate that remarkable love every time we gather.

Dr. John Sams, who has spent his life working for the American Leprosy Mission, visited our church once and told some interesting stories. One of the stories was about a woman and her husband who had gone to Thailand as missionaries in 1902. They lived in the same house until 1954, when Dr. and Mrs. Sams came to relieve them. Some ti:ne before the Samses arrived, the husband died. Just before the Samses had arrived to relieve the woman, now a widow, she had been sent to be examined by a leprosy specialist. That specialist had given her the sad news that she had contracted leprosy. Shortly after receiving the news, the woman had come back to the house where she had lived with her late husband for fifty-two years. With great sadness, she slowly climbed the stairs of the house where she had spent more than half a century serving the Lord. When she reached the top floor she met Mrs. Sams, a loving, caring woman who took her into her arms. The older woman almost collapsed with emotion. She responded, saying, "I didn't think I would ever be hugged again."

Isn't that what each of us needs when we are brought low by the burdens of this life and the things that we have to endure? Isn't our greatest need to have a loving God put his arms of love around us? That is the kind of God that we have. That is God who is revealed in Jesus Christ.

When I was growing up, I was exposed to some people who made it hard to believe in a loving God. They did not tell me about a God who was going to be so *for* me that he would lay down his own Son's life. They didn't tell me there wasn't anything I could do that would make God love me any less than he loved me right then. They did not tell me that the thing that would finally break me down and make me want to be a Christian was not the threat of God but the love of God. Who is going to bring any charge against God's elect?

Confidence Is Knowing That Jesus Defends Us

Then Paul asked this question, "Is it Christ Jesus who is going to bring the charges?" That would be Jesus' right, for he is the only perfect man who ever lived. He faced all our temptations and did not yield. He surely sees the warts on us and knows all our failures. Then Paul answered his own question: "How could Jesus bring any charges against his people when he has chosen to take his place at the right hand of Almighty God? He sits in the place of supremacy and makes intercession for his people." In other words, Jesus intercedes for us now, and he is our advocate and our defense attorney in the world to come. Now, if Jesus doesn't bring any charges, who could possibly bring any charges against God's people?

Paul is using legal terminology; he sets the stage in the courthouse, and he argues, "If Jesus Christ is your defense attorney, who is going to make any charge against you?" Would you worry about a prosecutor if you had a defense attorney like Perry Mason? If the scriptwriters hadn't been so ingenious in the ways they had Perry win all those cases, viewers would have been so bored they would have switched channels. The poor old prosecutor lost, lost, lost week after week. It is the same thing Paul is describing here. Why are you worried about charges being brought against you?

Confidence Is Knowing That Nothing Can Separate Us from God

When God is for you, certainly you live this life with confidence. There is nothing in this life that can break you down. You may face disappointment; you may be treated like sheep going to the slaughter, but nothing will separate you from the love of Christ. Paul writes in Romans 8:35, "Will hardship, or distress, or persecution, or famine, or nakedness, or peril, or sword?" He starts with the smallest tribulation and argues to the greatest, which is the sword. Paul himself died by the sword.

We cannot think, ask, or wish for any more than that. Paul was not talking about some tribulation at the end of time that is supposed to be catastrophic. He was referring to tribulation that really means "grinding." He was talking about the daily business of living. People talk about the "daily grind," and that is what Paul was talking about; it can really wear us down and chew us up. Somebody said to me the other day, "The problem with my days is that they are so everlastingly daily." The daily grind has a way of revealing the sons and daughters of God and separating the wheat from the chaff.

In Matthew 13:24, Jesus tells of a man who went out and sowed some good seed in his field. Then, while everyone was sleeping, an enemy came and sowed weeds among the wheat. When the servants went out and saw the weeds among the good wheat, they went to the master and said, "Don't you want us to pull up those old weeds?" The master said, "No, you can't pull them up because you might pull up the good wheat along with the bad. You let them grow together and let them live together until the harvesttime, and then I'll separate them." There is something about grinding over a period of years that separates. Some people's sins are obvious now, and the whole world can see them. Some people's sins are obvious later. But there is nothing that can grind down a believer.

It was Ian MacLaren who said that we should not fear suffering. He said that Christians do not fear suffering because our Lord Jesus Christ has left a kiss on the lip of the cup of suffering. We will not shrink from the cup because Jesus has drunk that cup. He has drunk it to its bitterest dregs, and he knows what we need to endure and even to triumph over it.

A mail carrier was asked why he enjoyed his work so much. He worked one little neighborhood with the same routine every day—just walking and delivering the mail. The mail carrier explained that what made his job great was the knowledge that he had all the resources of a great country behind him. He said that if necessary, he could call out all of the federal forces, all of the police powers of the strongest nation in the world, and they would come to his aid to help him deliver a single postcard.

There is another who is so great that, in comparison, all the nations of the world appear as a single drop in the bucket. But God, according to this scripture, makes all his resources available to his people when they need them. Who could ask, wish, or hope for more than that?

Paul declares that nothing can separate us from the love of God in Christ Jesus, not even death (Rom. 8:39). Death cannot separate us because Christ died and was resurrected. Christ preceded us into that experience.

How do you handle thoughts of your own death? When my father died, I was still quite young, and I remember thinking I would not be as afraid to die anymore because my grandmother, my grandfather, and now my father had gone through that experience. If they could endure it, I knew I could, too. But it was a kind of resignation to the acceptance of the inevitable. It wasn't until later that, somehow, I realized that Jesus conquered death. Jesus, whose death was the death of deaths, preceded me into death. Because he has gone into a dark and scary unknown, all the dread has been taken out of the darkness for me.

I had an experience early on that helped me understand something of the hope and the confidence of Christ's resurrection. It happened for us at our house during what I call "replacement therapy." Replacement therapy is when one of your children's pets dies and you get another pet. In our case, a cat had died, and so we went out right away to get another pet for our youngest daughter, Cathy. She selected a tiny peekapoo puppy. The task was given to me to build the house in which the dog would live. The only kind of dog I knew very much about was a really big bird dog, so when I built the doghouse (unaccustomed as I am to building anything),

I built a very large house. It was so large, so cavernous, that it scared the little peekapoo. He would not go near it. We would put his food in there, and he would go hungry; we would put his water in there, and he would go thirsty. In exasperation I would shove him in and hold my hands over the door; but the minute I would move, he would run out, unbelievably frightened.

Finally, I gave up in disgust, went inside, and sat down in the den, leaving Cathy to cry about her dad's impatience and the refusal of her puppy to cooperate. After a time, Cathy got down on her hands and knees and crawled into the doghouse. When she crawled into the doghouse, something really wonderful happened. That little puppy just trotted right in beside her and stretched out on the doghouse floor. Soon he was taking a nap. Suddenly all the shadows stood still for him, and all the dread was taken out of the darkness, because the one whom he loved and trusted had preceded him into that dark and frightening place. Now it no longer caused him to fear.

Jesus said, "Do not let your hearts be troubled. Believe in God, believe also in me. In my Father's house there are many dwelling places. If it were not so, would I have told you that I go to prepare a place for you? And if I go to prepare a place for you, I will come again and will take you to myself, so that where I am, there you may be also" (John 14:1-3).

Just as death cannot separate us because Christ has died, so also life cannot separate us because Christ has risen. In his rising, Christ has offered himself to us through his Holy Spirit that makes intercession for us, walking with us every step of the way and making available all the resources that are in God. There is nothing in my pilgrimage or in my death, whether I live or whether I die, that will change the fact that I am the Lord's. This is the way Paul said it: "Neither angels nor principalities, those great forces of wickedness and the invisible forces that come against us, nor nothing in time or space can come between us. Neither the things that are present nor the things to come, nothing we encounter in this life and certainly not in the last judgment of things to come, should we fear. Whatever is to come, Christ will be there to receive us, to stand beside us, and to claim us as his own. Neither height nor depth nor anything else in all creation can separate us."

It is interesting to think about height and depth, isn't it? In reality, sometimes we handle the depths better than we do the heights. When some people come to an easy time in their lives, they are so loaded with shame and guilt that they cannot embrace the good. They consider it an illusion, and they cannot believe themselves to be so blessed.

Sometimes in the marriage ceremony, when I say, "for better or for worse," I recognize that many people will endure the worse but cannot handle the better. During prosperity and the easy times, they seem to lose their sense of focus, their dependence upon God. But thanks be to God, neither height nor depth can separate us from God—nothing in all of creation. Indeed, he said that we are conquerors but not just conquerors: "We are more than conquerors through him who loved us"

(Rom. 8:37). Another translation says that we are "super conquerors" in Jesus Christ.

Not long ago a super conqueror was commended to God. Gene Hines had been a church member for forty-one years, and many friends and members of his Sunday school class gathered to be a part of the service for him. The last time I talked to him he said, "Bill, there have been eight times in the last twenty-five years when I have heard the doctors say to me, 'I am afraid you have a malignancy.' Now I weigh ninety-five pounds. I cannot eat; I cannot even swallow." A few days later, Gene was gone. Some people say cancer got him. But you cannot persuade those of us wo knew him that cancer conquered him. Those of us who sat at his bedside and wrote down the order of his service, those who listened to him talk about God's grace, cannot be persuaded that cancer got him. Cancer may have been the thing that brought him at last to the transition to the next life. But nothing conquered him.

We are more than conquerors in Jesus Christ, for we are persuaded that the God who gave his only Son will save us, protect us, and deliver us; and that is the root and the foundation of all of our confidence. We can say with Isaiah,

> The mountains may depart
>   and the hills be removed,
> but my steadfast love shall not
>   depart from you,
> and my covenant of peace
>   shall not be removed,
> says the LORD, who has
>   compassion on you. (Isa. 54:10)

And our confidence is sure when we read,

> When you pass through the
>   waters, I will be with you;
> and through the rivers, they
>   shall not overwhelm you;
> when you walk through fire you
>   shall not be burned,
>   and the flame shall not
>   consume you. . . .
> Because you are precious in my
>   sight,
> and honored, and I love you. (Isa. 43:2, 4*a*)

In the strength of that love, we live with confidence.

11.

With Power

In the first book, Theophilus, I wrote about all that Jesus did and taught from the beginning until the day when he was taken up to heaven, after giving instructions through the Holy Spirit to the apostles whom he had chosen. After his suffering he presented himself alive to them by many convincing proofs, appearing to them during forty days and speaking about the kingdom of God. While staying with them, he ordered them not to leave Jerusalem, but to wait there for the promise of the Father. "This," he said, "is what you have heard from me; for John baptized with water, but you will be baptized with the Holy Spirit not many days from now."

So when they had come together, they asked him, "Lord, is this the time when you will restore the kingdom to Israel?" He replied, "It is not for you to know the times or periods that the Father has set by his own authority. But you will receive power when the Holy Spirit has come upon you; and you will be my witnesses in Jerusalem, in all Judea and Samaria, and to the ends of the earth."

ACTS 1:1-8

When the day of Pentecost had come, they were all together in one place. And suddenly from heaven there came a sound like the rush of a violent wind, and it filled the entire house where they were sitting. Divided tongues, as of fire, appeared among them, and a tongue rested on each of them. All of them were filled with the Holy Spirit and began to speak in other languages, as the Spirit gave them ability.

Now there were devout Jews from every nation under heaven living in Jerusalem. And at this sound the crowd gathered and was bewildered, because each one heard them speaking in the native language of each. Amazed and astonished, they asked, "Are not all these who are speaking Galileans? And how is it that we hear, each of us, in our own native language?"

ACTS 2:1-8

———————— 🌱 ————————

One of the highlights of a recent trip to Egypt was an opportunity to see King Tut's treasures in the Antiquities Museum. Those who have seen the halls full of treasure that was taken from King Tut's tomb know that each item carries its own fascination. Two things in particular caught my attention. I was intrigued by a number of walking canes that had been carved for the young king, and by the footstool on which his feet rested while sitting on the throne. Each cane had an image of an enemy carved into the handle. In a similar manner, the faces of the king's enemies had been carved into the top of his footstool. When the king picked up his cane, he held his enemy in his hand. When he sat down on his throne, he put his enemies under his feet.

Wouldn't it be wonderful if there were some power available to us that would enable us to put our enemies under out feet, to get on top of life instead of having life get on top of us? Jesus said, "You will receive power when the Holy Spirit has come upon you" (Acts 1:8).

Along with Christmas, Pentecost is one of the most important festivals of the church year. Christmas marks the coming of Jesus in the flesh, and Pentecost marks the birthday of the church, when the people of God received Jesus Christ risen from the dead, present within them through the power of the Holy Spirit.

If the church of Jesus Christ had a missing persons bureau, at the head of the list would be the third person of the Holy Trinity. The doctrine of the Holy Spirit is perhaps one of the most neglected teachings in the Bible. Luke, who wrote the history of the early church, tells us in the beginning of the Acts of the Apostles that in his first work, the Gospel of Luke, he has dealt with all the things that Jesus said and did during his life here on this earth. Now he says he is going to talk about a new dimension, the promise of the Father; namely, the Holy Spirit.

We Must Be Willing to Wait for Power

Our Lord knew how important it was for his people to be filled with his Spirit. He told the anxious disciples, "Do not leave Jerusalem until you receive the promise of the Father, the presence of the Holy Spirit." How difficult it must have been for them to wait!

Waiting has been hard for every generation and certainly for our generation. We are the ones who put signs in our offices stating, "If I had wanted it tomorrow, I would have ordered it tomorrow." We are the "now generation." We want split-second results. The split second is the interval between the time the traffic light turns green and the person in the car behind you blows the horn.

I still remember the radio announcer who said, before the war with Iraq, "Listen, we know it is going to be nasty; we know many people are going to die, but let's get on with it." We were reared on TV sitcoms, microwave dinners, and instant coffee; and we believe that anything, even dying, is better than waiting. Waiting is tough. We see waiting as a kind of dying. It is giving in to inactivity, or avoiding action.

Recently, some friends and I visited a Confederate cemetery that is adjacent to a church that was used as a hospital during the Civil War. Thirty-three Confederate soldiers are buried there. One day, in the children's sermon, a minister at that church was telling the boys and girls about the thirty-three soldiers who died in those very pews. The minister said, "They died in the service right here on these pews." One little boy asked, "Was it in the 9:00 o'clock or the 11:00 o'clock service?"

That is why a lot of people don't like church. They can't come to church because they don't want to just sit and be still. For them, the church is where the action isn't. Nothing is happening, and they are looking for action.

It is not easy for this generation to wait. And yet, Jesus is indicating that until we learn to wait, we will not have any power in our lives.

Waiting is the key to power. When we wait, the Bible says through Paul, "[We] can do all things through Christ who strengthens [us]" (Phil. 4:13). The Bible says that God has not given us a spirit of fear and timidity. God has given us a spirit of love and power and self-control. Paul wrote to the church in Corinth, which had given him so much trouble, "I am going to come and check on you, and when I come, I don't want to hear noise. I don't want to know anything about your fancy words; I want to see your power." But waiting is tough because it is an acknowledgment of our inadequacy. It is another way of saying we aren't ready.

We Must Admit Our Powerlessness

The disciples were not ready for the power of the Holy Spirit, even after they had studied three years with Jesus, even after they had heard all of his stories and watched all of his miracles and then had it "made real" by seeing him come back from the dead. He appeared to them behind closed doors, met them on the beach, and even cooked their breakfast on the beach. The disciples had seen Jesus appear to five hundred people at one time; Jesus demonstrated everything he had ever said and taught, and still they weren't ready.

It goes against the grain to acknowledge that we need outside help, doesn't it? But there are some things over which we are powerless. There are some things we cannot handle. The Bible states that the first step toward gaining power is to acknowledge our inadequacy. We really need some outside help. Somehow, when we finally grasp that realization and turn to God, good things begin to happen.

One of the premises of Alcoholics Anonymous and many other groups like it is that the individual must first have the ability to acknowledge inadequacy or powerlessness. I know a man who has been sober for 8,774 days. He doesn't reduce it to months, and he can't even talk about years. You see, he has learned to live one day at a time. He helps people who are struggling with problems like his. He goes to the Harbor House to work with them, and en route he always stops at the dough-nut shop to get some fresh doughnuts and a cup of coffee.

One day he decided that the people at the Har-bor House would like some of those doughnuts. He bought a variety of doughnuts and took them with him. He said it was like having the sacrament when he shared those doughnuts and coffee. He said that the last thing they do in one of their meet-ings is to come out in the middle of the room in a huddle, just like a sports team. Together they clasp hands as a team and sing "Lean on Me." When they finish singing, they stand up with a shout and are ready to go out and face the challenge of another day.

You are not really ready to live until you realize that everybody is a "leaner." The difference between a healthy person and an unhealthy person is that the healthy person learns where to find strength and on whom to *lean*.

The first step in reaching for power is to recognize our own inadequacies. That is hard for many of us. We are impatient and hasty, and it shows in the qual-ity of our lives. We are not good at waiting because too many of us live on the edge of life. We have run it all the way out to the edge of the paper. We don't have any good, healthy margins around our physical or our spiritual resources, or even our economic or our emotional resources. We "live it to the limit," as it were. We don't have anything left. We don't have any reserves upon which we can call. It takes everything we have for us to keep on going. One of the expressions I hear most often is, "I am drained. There isn't anything else left to give."

One museum exhibit depicts a primitive steam engine, one of the first developed in this country. There is a breakdown of all the wheels and other components that went into making that locomotive. And this amazing information is furnished: 96 percent of its power was consumed in propelling itself, leaving only 4 percent to pull the load.

I know people like that—I am like that sometimes myself. Everyday living exhausts so much of our physical, mental, and spiritual resources that we have very little left over to pull the load, to be there to give strength emotionally or spiritually to anybody else. We start stiff-arming people, and we start stringing barbed wire. We cannot take on any more baggage.

Even in the community of Jesus Christ, we sometimes can't take on somebody else's problem because we are so preoccupied with our own problems. It takes everything we have just to get from here to there. We fail to admit our own powerlessness.

To be a Christian is to be a powerful person, because being a Christian involves a relationship with the Holy Spirit. Sometimes we act as though God is at the root of our problem, when at the heart is an unacknowledged inadequacy. We can't get rid of that old entrepreneurial spirit that makes us play games with one another, and so we keep saying, "I can handle it. I can manage it." The truth of the matter is evident for all to see: we cannot handle it, and we cannot manage it.

We are like that servant Jesus described in the twenty-fifth chapter of Matthew. He told about the man going into a far country who left what he had with his servants. He gave the first one five talents; the second one two talents; and the last one, one talent. When the master came back from the far country, he checked on how each had done with his talents. The one who had been given five talents had multiplied them; he had five more. The one who had been given two talents had multiplied his. Then that poor creature who had received one talent brought his back to the master, still wrapped in a napkin with dirt on it. He had buried it in the earth. When the master asked him why he had done such a thing, he said, "I know you to be a hard man. I know you are unreasonable, and so I just hid it for safekeeping." In other words, "You just expect too much of me, God." That is the testimony of someone who relies on only his native ability, on his intelligence, and on his education, and doesn't take into consideration the promise of God to be there and to make the difference. Leave it to natural ability alone, and everything in the Gospels has a ring of unreasonableness about it.

Jesus said to the people, "Which of you who has a servant out plowing or tending the sheep will say to that servant after he has been out there all day, 'Go in and fix yourself some supper'?" In those days, they did not plow from 9:00 A.M. to 5:00 P.M.; they went from can to can't. They did not plow in an air-conditioned tractor; they wrestled with a pair of yoked oxen.

Jesus said, "Which master will say to the servant, 'Hey! I am all rested. I have been sitting here on the front porch just cooling it in my rocking chair all day, and I know you are really worn out. You go in there and fix yourself some supper, and don't worry about me; I'll just have some soup'?" Jesus said, "You won't do that. You'll say to that man, 'I know you are tired, but gird yourself; reach down into your reservoir and get a little something extra. You go in there and fix my supper, draw my bath, turn back my bed, and lay out my pajamas; and after you have tucked me in, then you go get yourself a peanut butter and jelly sandwich.' But before you go to sleep tonight, you fall on your knees and say, 'O God, have mercy on me, I have just been doing my duty.'"

You thought God was reasonable? Paul said, "I appeal to you therefore, brothers and sisters, by the mercies of God, to present your bodies as a living sacrifice, holy and acceptable to God, which is your spiritual worship" (Rom. 12:1). Jesus said, "I send you out as lambs in the midst of ravenous wolves, and, as far as I am concerned, you are wolf bait. I'll send you out there to get beat to a nubbin by the world, but don't worry about it; I'll put you back together in the world to come."

Why does the gospel sound so unreasonable? Why is it that we only expect a few to take it seriously? Could it be because we are in the same quandary as those disciples at Ephesus?

We Must Receive the Holy Spirit

The nineteenth chapter of Acts tells us that when Paul went to Ephesus, he met with the Christians there and asked, "Did you receive the Holy Spirit when you first believed?" You see, he discovered something was missing there. They replied, "We didn't even know there was a Holy Spirit." Paul said, "Well, into what were you baptized?" They said, "The baptism of John." The apostle probably threw up his hands as he said, "The baptism of John is a water baptism. I am talking about a baptism by fire, a baptism by the Holy Spirit."

Some still have the old premise of bootstrap theology: "I'll do my best; I'll make a commitment; I'll work hard; I'll do this thing if it kills me." The apostle Paul said, "On your knees, folks, we are going to have a prayer meeting right now. We are going to pray for the power of the Holy Spirit, because Christians don't have to live their lives with an 'ought to' mentality, with a sense of duty only and the feeling that real discipleship is only for a privileged few. Disciples can fulfill the requirements of Christ while they sing."

The Holy Spirit was described on Pentecost as fire and as wind. The same frightened disciples who had run away and deserted Jesus took to the streets after Pentecost with great boldness. They miraculously spoke so that all could understand in their own languages. They preached so powerfully and so courageously that the authorities accused them of being drunk. Three thousand people were converted by a single sermon in a single day.

The Greek word for power is *dynamis*. That is the word from which we get our word *dynamite*. The root word of the French word for power means "to be able." To receive the Holy Spirit is to be able. It doesn't mater how superbly trained you are; another technique will not do it. It doesn't matter how much you know. It doesn't matter about your natural ability. You are not ready to face life with all of its complexities until you have the gift of the Holy Spirit.

Let me tell you about the author Annie Dillard and her experience on board a ship one day. She saw a moth that reminded her of a hummingbird. It had a large, thick body and tiny wings. She saw the moth resting on the railing of the ship anchored near the shore. It was "panting," because that particular moth cannot fly with such a heavy body and tiny wings until it supercharges its muscles with oxygen. For the moth, just idly waiting is not enough preparation. Dillard ran to her cabin to get some paper to draw a picture of the moth, and when she came back, it was panting even more heavily. The moth was trying to prepare itself to fly. Pathetically and erratically it started out, up and down, up and down, each time a little lower. Finally she saw the poor moth as it drowned in the ocean. It tried to fly before it was ready.

The waiting the Bible talks about is not sitting idly by, but, like that panting moth, hungering and thirsting after righteousness. It is praying expectantly as the disciples did. It is learning to do what the Lord has commanded us to do. In all these ways we are waiting. Christ will surely keep his promise, and we will be filled with power that we might be effective witnesses for his sake.

12.

With Boldness

While Peter and John were speaking to the people, the priests, the captain of the temple, and the Sadducees came to them, much annoyed because they were teaching the people and proclaiming that in Jesus there is the resurrection of the dead. So they arrested them and put them in custody until the next day, for it was already evening. But many of those who heard the word believed; and they numbered about five thousand.

The next day their rulers, elders, and scribes assembled in Jerusalem, with Annas the high priest, Caiaphas, John, and Alexander, and all who were of the high-priestly family. When they had made the prisoners stand in their midst, they inquired, "By what power or by what name did you do this?" Then Peter, filled with the Holy Spirit, said to them, "Rulers of the people and elders, if we are questioned today because of a good deed done to someone who was sick and are asked how this man has been healed, let it be known to all of you, and to all the people of Israel, that this man is standing before you in good health by the name of Jesus Christ of Nazareth, whom you crucified, whom God raised from the dead.

This Jesus is
> *'the stone that was rejected by you, the builders; it has become the cornerstone.'*

There is salvation in no one else, for there is no other name under heaven given among mortals by which we must be saved."

Now when they saw the boldness of Peter and John and realized that they were uneducated and ordinary men, they were amazed and recognized them as companions of Jesus. When they saw the man who had been cured standing beside them, they had nothing to say in opposition.

ACTS 4:1-14

We have some ambiguities about boldness in our day. Some boldness we respect, but there are other types that we do not respect. We do not, for instance, respect that boldness that is marked by a kind of reckless abandon, a boldness that does not take into consideration the factors involved but simply moves forward without thinking. That kind of boldness does not draw us; rather, it repels us.

Then there is that boldness that is characteristic of one who cares neither for limb nor property. We do not admire that kind of boldness; instead, we are afraid of it, and rightfully so. Some boldness is defined as unduly forward or brazen. We do not appreciate those who practice that kind of boldness; rather, we distance ourselves from them.

But there is a finer brand of boldness that is characteristic of one who has made a realistic appraisal of all the factors involved—one who counts the cost and then moves forward. This person does not pretend to be without fear but, after having calculated the cost, goes forward anyway.

In his classic *Moby Dick*, Herman Melville illustrated this concept as they were searching for the great whale. Officer Starbuck makes a speech in which he says that he will not have any man in the boat with him who is not afraid of a whale. It is all right to be afraid. We are to count the cost and to realistically appraise the situation. That old saying about sawing is true in every case—we measure twice but we cut only once.

Count the Cost and Then Move Forward

One scholar has referred to the appearance of the apostles Peter and John before the council as one of the greatest demonstrations of courage the world has ever known. Those who witnessed the appearance and the speech of those uneducated Galileans described their demeanor in one word. They called it boldness. Boldness typified everything they did.

Simon Peter counted the cost, and then he became like that Greek warrior Achilles, who was told before a certain battle that he would surely die if he went forward. Achilles counted the cost and said that he must go on, nevertheless. That is the kind of boldness demonstrated in the book of Acts by the disciples.

It is tough to be bold when you are in the position they faced. Their lives were hanging in the balance.

They knew full well that the council that examined them that day was the very same council of seventy-one elders and renowned rabbis and chief priests that only a few days earlier had condemned their Lord and Master, Jesus Christ, to death. They understood that, because they had created such a stir by healing the crippled man and by converting three thousand people in one meeting, this council was threatened and would like to be rid of them. The disciples knew what was hanging in the balance, but they were bold anyway.

Overcome the Fear of Embarrassment

It was tough for the disciples, not only because their lives were in jeopardy, but also because they were threatened with public embarrassment. In many ways, public embarrassment is more threatening than death. A recent poll indicates that there are many people who are less afraid of death than they are of having to make a public speech. Many people are terrified at the idea of having to stand up in front of a crowd. They have nightmares about such things.

Peter and John were held in contempt by the members of this council because they were considered ignorant and unlearned. By the standards of the council, they were. Peter and John had no technical education; they had no professional qualifications—nothing to commend them in the eyes of this august body.

The members of that council sat there in an imposing semicircle, shaped like a horseshoe. Peter and

John stood at the bottom of that horseshoe so that every eye was focused upon them. They were confronted by the wealthiest, the most intellectual, the most powerful people in that nation. Peter and John were expected to speak in the middle of that hostility and intellectual snobbery.

Nobody likes a snob of any kind, but if we were to run a poll about snobs, intellectual snobs might be at the top of the list. These are people who somehow feel that because of a few degrees, a few letters after their names, their feet don't quite touch the ground and they are better than everybody else. We like to see them get their "comeuppance."

There is a story of an incident that probably took place on U.S. 17, that highway along the east coast of our country starting way up north and going all the way to Miami. Before the interstates were built, U.S. 17 was a very popular highway, and the tourists filled that road to Miami and back again. As the tourists drove through the southeastern part of our country, they stopped at many of the places the papers call "clip joints"—maybe a monkey farm or a reptile farm or something like that.

One day one of the tourists had toured one of those attractions, and as he was coming out, he turned to a local citizen who was whittling as he leaned against the tree. The tourist asked, "Tell me, friend, isn't it true that the people in this area are very backward?" The man thought a moment and said, "Well, I guess we are, but I ain't never seen any of us spend $10 to tour an alligator farm."

You can be intimidated by an intellectual snob. Peter and John were men with no credentials as they stood before that council, and the council simply wanted them to speak in order that they might embarrass themselves, that they might reveal their lack of intelligence. The authorities asked, "In what name, by what power, did you do this?" Even the magicians had names in their incantations. They had to have some magic against which to draw, and now the council inquired of Peter and John, "What's behind your act?"

Simon Peter stood up strong and tall and answered, "We want all of you rulers of Israel to know that it was in the name of Jesus, whom you crucified, whom God raised from the dead, that this man was healed. Furthermore, there is no other name under heaven by which you can be saved."

Simon Peter became exclusive, you see, and he upset all those easy-going people who are constantly saying, "Well, one religion is as good as the other." The council called an instant recess. "What is going on here? These men are bold," they said.

Act Boldly, Even When It's Not Convenient

It was tough for Peter and John to witness, and it is tough for us to be bold in our time, too, isn't it? We don't have to try to put ourselves in the position of Peter and John and say, "What would I have done?" You can raise that question about your workplace, your play place, or anywhere you go. You can raise the question, "Do I own the name of Jesus Christ?" Even in the little ways, do I acknowledge Jesus in a country that is becoming more violent and more secular all the time?

It is not easy to be bold. We can only ask ourselves if we claim Christ in all the times and places and opportunities that we have. Sometimes it just isn't convenient or expedient.

A minister friend of mine was faced with a thorny decision soon after he began a new assignment. A member of the church had died, and he had stipulated in his will that $25,000 should be given to the church. Members of his family planned to contest the will because they had been excluded. To make the situation even more difficult, the deceased member had marked through a portion of his will, therefore rendering its legality suspect. The unhappy members of the family offered to let the estate be settled if the church would give them half of the money. If the church refused, the family threatened to take the matter to court.

The minister met with the Board of Trustees, whom he hardly knew, to try to resolve the issue. An attorney who was present advised the trustees to take the family's offer. "There is a good chance that we might lose the court battle," the attorney explained. The minister and half of the trustees disagreed, maintaining that the church should honor the integrity of the man's intent. Obviously, the man who had died had intended to give the bulk of his modest estate to the church.

The dissident family members made good on their threat and took the issue to court; they took it all the way to the state supreme court. The supreme court ruled in favor of the church. Later the trustees met to celebrate the victory that had been won for the church. One of the members exclaimed, "I wish we could have put a million dollars at risk. It would have meant even more to all of us."

Putting something at risk is not easy; it requires considerable courage. Holy boldness should be the characteristic of a Christian. "God did not give us a spirit of cowardice, but rather a spirit of power and of love and of self-discipline" (II Tim. 1:7). Timidity isn't a Christian virtue; rather, boldness is a Christian virtue. Where does it come from? How do you become bold like Peter and John?

Discover God's Promise

Boldness comes when you realize God keeps his promises. As Simon Peter stood before the council, he remembered, Jesus' words while he was still with them in the flesh: "Don't you be anxious when they haul you before the council, because when you stand before the council I will give you the words to say. When you speak, it will not be you who speaks; it will be the spirit of your Father who speaks through you." In that day, by his own personal experience, Simon Peter experienced the fulfillment of God's promise. When you talk to someone who has experienced the fulfillment of God's promise, you are talking to a person who has discovered boldness.

I heard a minister friend give his retirement speech one night at a reception before a group of pastors. Many of us had admired this minister and the boldness that characterized his work with young preachers across the years. He said, "I want to tell you one thing as I retire. I want to tell you, God keeps his promises." When you know that, deep down inside, it makes a profound difference in the way you relate to other people in this world and the way you do things.

The key to holy boldness is to be filled with the Holy Spirit. Peter and John had been with Jesus; but there is something better than having been with Jesus, and that is Jesus being with you now through the Holy Spirit.

There are many people who have been with Jesus who never darken the door of the church, who never claim the name of Jesus Christ. They will tell you how they had perfect attendance at church for years. They will tell you how they have been with Jesus. But where are they when Jesus needs them?

I'd sooner build a fire with cold ashes than try to resurrect someone who had an experience forty years ago and hasn't seen or talked to the Lord since then. Simon Peter was so full of Jesus, so full of the Holy Spirit, that there simply was not any room for fear.

I remember a story that came out of Rome before Christianity was accepted as a religion. The Romans decided to eradicate the Christians; they certainly wanted the Christians out of the army. According to this old story, they marched a particular group of soldiers out into the wilderness during a harsh winter day. The captain said, "All of you who are Christians step forward," and ten men acknowledged their faith in Christ. They were then stripped of their warm uniforms, and their uniforms were placed beside a roaring fire. The ten soldiers were then made to march a short distance from the fire, and they were to stand there until they were ready to renounce their faith in Christ.

As the Christians stood there, slowly freezing to death in the bitter cold and snow, they began to chant, "Ten soldiers witnessing for Christ." As the hours passed, they grew weaker and weaker, and finally the chanting changed to, "Nine soldiers witnessing for Christ." One had not died, but rather something within that one had died, and he was crawling pitifully in the direction of the fire and his warm uniform.

An amazing thing happened at that point in the story. Another soldier, one standing by the fire, stripped off his uniform and joined the other nine in the freezing cold, saying with a strong voice, "Ten soldiers witnessing for Christ."

That's what we need today. We need Christians who will boldly witness for Christ, no matter the circumstances, no matter the place. We need Christians who say, "Lead on, O King eternal, we follow, not with fears."